AND WHAT'S SO FUNNY THIS TIME?

Larry Wilde, the funniest, most irreverent, best-selling jokester in this world, gets some great laughs on the Jews, again, in his LAST (maybe, next to the last) OFFICIAL JEWISH JOKE BOOK.

With more than 4½ million of his joke books sold, Larry Wilde has already exposed the funny side of the Democrats, the Irish, Italians and Poles, Blacks, Virgins and Golfers . . . So who's next?

After the uproarious, hilarious success of THE OFFICIAL JEWISH JOKE BOOK, Larry Wilde's back with more.

GET READY FOR *MORE* LARRY WILDE
JOKE BOOKS,
COMING SOON FROM BANTAM BOOKS.

THE
LAST
OFFICIAL
JEWISH
JOKE
BOOK
(Maybe, next to the last!)

Larry Wilde

Illustrations by Ron Wing

BANTAM BOOKS
TORONTO · NEW YORK · LONDON · SYDNEY

THE LAST OFFICIAL JEWISH JOKE BOOK
A Bantam Book/November 1980

Illustrated by Ron Wing.

ISBN 0-553-14349-2

Published simultaneously in the United States and Canada

PRINTED IN THE UNITED STATES OF AMERICA

0 9 8 7 6 5 4 3 2

For Morty Bass—
the lovable manufacturer
of Jeri Morton Lingerie

When you're hungry, sing!
When you're hurt, laugh!

—JEWISH FOLK SAYING

One hot summer day, Mrs. Superfein took her little boy, Alan, to Jones Beach.

CONTENTS

Introduction

If you prick us, do we not bleed?
If you tickle us, do we not laugh?

WILLIAM SHAKESPEARE
The Merchant of Venice

Spoken by Shylock these lines, written almost 400 years ago, underscore two key aspects of the Jews as a people—their suffering and persecution throughout history and their ability to survive tragedy through humor.

Jews were the first to initiate gags that were self-deprecating; they gave birth to ethnic humor. After all, since everyone else was making fun of them, they figured they might as well get in on a good thing.

This talent to laugh at themselves is rooted in a fierce determination to persevere in spite of harsh treatment by their fellow men. The following story can best illustrate the point:

During the Nazi reign of terror in Germany Horowitz was dragged from his tailor shop in Berlin by two burly Gestapo men. After roughing him up one of the Germans said, "Who was responsible for our defeat in World War One?"

"The Jews and the pretzel makers," replied the little tailor.

One of the Nazis scratched his head and asked, "Why the pretzel makers?"

"Why the Jews?"

Nathan Ausabel points out in his *Treasury of Jewish Folklore*, "Jews are skillful at joke-making because they are also virtuosi in the art of pathos." This laughter through tears philosophy became a defense mechanism and has enabled Jews to maintain a balanced outlook at life.

The Semitic view of society's incongruities makes us laugh. The next story pinpoints the essence of this special sense of humor, a situation seen through Jewish eyes:

Rabinowitz was staying at a plush Miami Beach hotel. He picked up the phone one morning and asked for room service.

"May I take your order," said a voice at the other end of the line.

"Yeah," snapped Rabinowitz. "I want three overdone fried eggs that are hard like a rock. Some burnt toast that you could hardly swallow and a cup of black coffee that tastes like mud."

"I'm sorry, sir," said room service. "We don't serve a breakfast like that."

"Oh, no? You did yesterday!"

Nothing is sacred to Jewish humor. Sex. Marriage. Mothers. Business. Death. The elderly. As long as fun is to be had, even five-thousand-year-old traditions come under comedic scrutiny:

CIRCUMCISION

*One way of sorting out
the mensch from the goys*

Jews were first to believe in one God and since they are comfortable in their theological beliefs it is not hard to be amused by matters religious. Roasting rabbis and the religion has long been comic fodder:

> *At a christening, the rabbi held the baby in his arms and asked, "Now, what is the little boy's name going to be?"*
>
> *"It ain't a little boy," said the grandmother. "You got hold of my thumb."*

In the Jewish "way" to evoke laughter you must not be direct. The listener is led innocently down the path and then, the punchline! Here's a typical example:

> *The Teitelbergs were at the airport terminal about to board a plane to Puerto Rico. This was their first vacation in years and they were very excited.*
>
> *"You know what," said the husband, "I really wish that we brought the piano."*
>
> *"What for?" asked Mrs. Teitelberg.*
>
> *"Because I left our tickets on it."*

It is not a coincidence that the majority of America's comedians and comedy writers are Jewish. Perhaps a special comic spirit is ingrained in Jews that lets them bring fun and happiness to others. How else could a story like this come about?

Two men were walking down the street when one of them said, "Hey, did you hear about the two Jewish guys who—"

"Hold it!" interrupted the other man. "Why does it always have to be two Jews? They've got enough trouble. Why don't you pick on some other nationality . . . like the Chinese?"

"Okay," said the first man. "These two Chinamen got off a bus and one said to the other, 'Tell me, Irving, when is your son getting Bar Mitzvahed?'"

THE LAST OFFICIAL JEWISH JOKE BOOK *(maybe, next to the last)* contains some of your old favorites but a whole lot more you've never heard before. Oh, what a collection! On every subject you can imagine. Listen, do me a favor. Sit down, have a glass of tea, maybe a Mallomar or a nice piece of honey cake . . . read a few pages. Believe me, before you turn around, you'll be laughing like a regular person.

LARRY WILDE

Los Angeles, 1980

Kibbitzers, Kvetches, & Klutzes

In Brooklyn, Eisenberg was awakened during the middle of the night by a phone call. The voice at the other end said, "Is this the residence of Thomas Nelson Bottomley Devonshire Cromwell, the Third?"

"*Oy, vey,* have you got the wrong number," chuckled Eisenberg.

* * *

At Grossinger's, the famous Catskill hotel, a couple sank down on the grass. "I love you," he murmured.

"But we just now met," she protested.

"I know," he answered. "But I'm only here for the weekend."

* * *

Mandel, a popular waiter at the old Lindy's Restaurant in New York passed away. Some of his show business regulars were so saddened by his loss that they decided to visit a medium to try and communicate with their lost buddy.

The medium advised, "Just knock on the table as you did when he was alive and he shall come forth."

The friends knocked on the table, but the old waiter did not appear. They knocked again and still no Mandel. Finally they banged and banged on the table and called his name.

Then, in a puff of smoke, Mandel appeared in his uniform with a cloth over his arm. One of his friends asked, "Why didn't you appear when you first heard us knocking?"

"It wasn't my table," answered the waiter.

* * *

Did you hear about Feldman, the dairy farmer?

He mated a golden Guernsey with a Holstein and created a new breed: the Goldstein.

Instead of "Moo" it says, "Nu!"

* * *

Delicatessen owner: Did you enjoy the food?

Bernheimer: I could get more nourishment biting my lip.

* * *

Miami Beach Lifeguard: I've been watching you
(To hotel guest)   for the last three days,
                        Mr. Coleman. You'll
                        have to stop urinating
                        in the pool.

Mr. Coleman: Everybody pees in the
                        pool.

Lifeguard: From the diving board?

* * *

In a Catskill hotel there was such a loud argument in one of the rooms that it could be heard all over the place.

"What's all the noise about?" asked a guest.

"They're having a battle of wits," said the desk clerk.

"A battle of wits?" asked the guest. "Who's in the room?"

"Markowitz, Berkowitz, and Hershkowitz!"

* * *

Abrams went on his first hunting trip. When he got back to New York his friend Hellman couldn't wait to hear about it.

"I went into the woods with the guide," said Abrams. "And two minutes later, I got lost. Suddenly, a big bear is standing right in front of me. I turned around and ran as fast as I could, but the bear was running even faster. Just when I feel his hot breath on my neck, he slipped and fell.

"I jumped over a brook and kept running, but there was the bear getting close to me again. He was almost on top of me, again he slipped and fell. I kept on running and finally I was in a clearing. The bear was coming fast and I didn't stand a chance. I saw the other hunters and shouted for help and just then the bear slipped and fell again. The guide then shot the bear and killed him."

"My God, you're a brave man," said Hellman. "If that would've happened to me, I would have made in my pants."

"What do you think the bear was slipping on?"

* * *

GENIUS

Average student with Jewish parents

* * *

Rose Eber, the Beverly Hills socialite breaks up Hadassah ladies with this lulu:

The Shapiros bought a twenty-five-room English Tudor mansion on Long Island and even brought over a butler from London. One day Mrs. Shapiro said to him, "Jeeves, this Sunday morning fix a brunch for four people in the dining room. The Lehmans are coming."

"Yes, Madam," replied Jeeves. "I shall see to it that the table looks splendid."

Sunday morning arrived and Mrs. Shapiro was astonished to see that eight places had been set at the dining table. "Hey, Jeeves," shouted Mrs. Shapiro. "I told you four, why you got places for eight?"

"Madam, the Lehmans phoned and said they're bringing the Bagels and the Bialys."

* * *

Hilliard, the big oilman from Houston, was visiting Miami Beach for the first time.

At Pumpernick's for lunch, he noticed a man at the next table had a plate of soup with two yellow balls.

The Texan asked his waitress what they were and she told him, "*matzoh* balls."

"Bring me a plate so's I can try 'em."

After he finished he told the waitress, "That sure tasted good! What other parts of the *matzoh* do you people cook?"

* * *

Sheckter's cousin Paul from Pittsburgh was visiting him in Staten Island. "What's the population here?" asked Paul. "Is everybody Jewish?"

"Well," said Sheckter, "we got about 30,000 Jews, maybe 3,000 Irish and Italian cops, firemen and garbage collectors. How is it in Pittsburgh?"

"Funny thing," replied Paul, "we got about 30,000 Jews, too, but about 150,000 gentiles."

"Say, that's some rich community!" said Sheckter. "You really need so many in help?"

* * *

"I'm gonna join the New York Athletic Club," said Nussbaum.

"Are you crazy or something?" replied Bloomberg. "That place is restricted. They ain't gonna take you."

"Well, you just wait. I'm goin' to England, take some diction lessons and I'm comin' back."

Nussbaum went to London. He studied for six months until no trace of his accent was apparent. He then showed up at the New York Athletic Club. "You wish to join?" asked the admissions officer.

"Yes," said Nussbaum.

"Where are you from?"

"England, of course!" said Nussbaum in perfect clipped English.

"Education?"

"Oxford."

"Children."

"Two. Wesley and Mallory. Wesley attends Smith. Mallory is at Harvard."

"Religion?"

"*Goy,* of course!"

* * *

Did you know that Manischewitz just bought out the Christian Wine Co.?

They're going to change the name to Manischaygetz.

* * *

Brickman and Krantz were invited out to dinner by their employer. During the course of the meal their host turned the subject of conversation to literature.

"Do you like Omar Khayyam?" he asked.

"Pretty good," said Brickman, "but personally, I prefer Mogen David sweet."

On the way home Krantz said to his friend: "Why don't you just say you don't know when you're asked something you don't understand? Omar Khayyam isn't a wine, you dummy! It's a cheese!"

* * *

A blacksmith, a woodchopper, and a Jew were masquerading in a harem as eunuchs but were quickly discovered when their erections showed under their robes. The sultan decided to punish them in accordance with their occupations. The blacksmith's penis was to be smashed with a hammer, the woodchopper's penis chopped off.

"I peddle lollypops," said the Jew. "If you don't mind, you could suck mine off!"

* * *

How can you tell a plain Jewish girl from a plain gentile girl?

By her fixed nose, capped teeth, false eyelashes, padded bra and blonde wig.

* * *

Ken Gerwit, Florida's popular *Peter Popavich* ladies' fashions prexy, breaks up buyers with this bauble:

Thalman, a wealthy clothing manufacturer, decided to give his son a Bar Mitzvah the Jewish world would never forget. The service was held in Madison Square Garden. Then the 2,000 guests were taken, driven to airplanes and flown to Africa for a safari.

There everybody was put on elephants and they headed into the jungle. Four hours later the whole caravan came to a sudden halt.

From the rear Thalman cried, "What's the hold up?"

The man in front also asked, "What's the hold up?" And the question was repeated 2,000 times till it reached the front of the procession.

The voice of the chief guide was heard: "We have to wait. There's another Bar Mitzvah passing through!"

* * *

A team of archaeologists were excavating in Israel when they came upon an ancient cave. Written on the wall of the cave were these symbols:

They could tell that the writings were at least three thousand years old. They chiseled the piece from the rock and had it brought to the museum where archaeologists from all over the world came to study the incredible find.

After months of conferences, the scholars held a huge meeting to discuss the meaning of the markings. The President of their society stood up, pointed at the first drawing and announced, "This looks like a tomato. We can judge that this was a hightly intelligent race as they knew how to grow things to eat. You can see the next drawing resembles a donkey, so obviously they were even smart enough to have animals help them till the soil. The next drawing looks like a shovel, which means they planted food. Then there is a fish which indicates that in famine when food didn't grow, they would take to the sea for nourishment. That last symbol appears to be the Star of David which means they were evidently Hebrews."

The audience applauded enthusiastically and the President said, "I'm glad you are in full agreement with our interpretations."

Suddenly Fleischer stood up in the back of the room and said, "I object to every word! The explanation of the markings is very simple. First of all, Jews don't read from left to right, but from right to left. Now, look again. It says, 'HOLY MACKEREL, DIG THE ASS ON THAT TO-MATO.' "

* * *

Klein and Rosen were having lunch. "It was the first time I ever went to a whorehouse," explained Klein.

"No kidding," said Rosen. "What was it like?"

"Well, Barbara, this beautiful blonde, came in wearing a negligee and carrying a small box. Out of the box she took a sugar doughnut and put it around my *putz*. On top of that she put whipped cream and maraschino cherries, and then ate it all off. It was sensational."

Rosen went to the same brothel, but Barbara was "busy." He was too excited to wait, so the madame provided him with Judy, a voluptuous Jewish brunette.

The next day the two friends met and Rosen told of the experience.

"She put a bagel around my *putz* and smothered it in cream cheese and lox."

"How did it feel?" asked Klein.

"I don't know. It looked so good, I ate it myself."

* * *

17

A Jewish actor had his nose straightened by a plastic surgeon. "How do you like it?" he asked a friend.

"Ah," said the friend. "A thing of beauty and a *goy* forever!"

* * *

RUSSIAN PROVERB

Knowledge is better than riches.

JEWISH TRANSLATION

We should all be as knowledgeable as Rothschild.

* * *

Did you hear about the new Miami Beach hotel that's so exclusive room service has an unlisted number?

* * *

"Do you have any children?"

"No."

"What do you do for aggravation?"

* * *

Dorf went into a New York deli. "Pastrami sandwich on rye," he ordered.

The waiter brought the sandwich. Dorf took one big bite and said. "What kind of sandwich is this?"

"You get what you order," said the waiter.

"The pastrami, okay, that's fine. But the bread is yesterday's."

"Whatsa matter?" said the waiter. "Yesterday wasn't a good day?"

* * *

OVERHEARD POOLSIDE IN THE CATSKILLS

"I was in Majorca on my vacation."

"Where's Majorca?"

"I don't know—we flew."

* * *

Gladys Altshuler, the gregarious Texas tycoon, tells this terrific titillater:

Marilyn was driving along a back road in upstate New York during a thunder and lightning storm when suddenly her car broke down. Looking for help, she came upon a deserted farmhouse and decided to spend the night there.

Just as she fell asleep a noise woke her. Standing over the bed was a man in a black cape baring two fanged teeth—a vampire. She grabbed the crucifix from around her neck and shoved it in his face, shouting, "The sign of the cross—you are powerless."

The vampire smiled and said, "*Sveetheart*, it *v*ouldn't help."

* * *

"Did you know Abraham Lincoln was Jewish?"

"Really?"

"Of course. Wasn't he shot in the temple?"

* * *

Bernard and Alvin were talking about their favorite subject. "You know how you're always judging girls on a scale of 1 to 10?" asked Alvin.

"Yeah," said Bernie.

"Well, what's a Jewish 10?"

"Dunno."

"That's a girl who's a 4—with 6 million dollars."

* * *

How did the Jews come to America?
Yidel by *Yidel.*

* * *

JEWISH PROVERB

It's no shame being poor. On the other hand, it's nothing to brag about either.

* * *

Marty Phillips, Bache's super stock market analyst, suggested this silly smiler:

Greenberg walked into his doctor's office and announced, "I would like to become a woman!"

"Are you crazy?" asked his physician.

"No," replied Greenberg. "I'd like to change my sex. Will you do the operation?"

"Absolutely not!" responded the doctor. "You'll have to go to Denmark!"

Greenberg went and six months later returned to the doctor's office. "I feel wonderful!" said Greenberg. "I function completely like a woman. In every way I am a female!"

"Don't you find you have any emotions or desires left over from being a man?"

"Well," said Greenberg, "I have to admit, that once in a while, in the morning, I get this great urge to lay *tefillin!*"

* * *

Sylvester sipped tea with his mom in a rear booth at Schraffts. He said, "Mother, Cedric and I have been very close friends for some time now. Well, I love Cedric and Cedric loves me. We wish to announce our engagement."

"Son," said the woman, "do you know what you're saying?"

"Yes, but I wouldn't dream of making a move without your blessing."

"But son, think what people will say, you cannot go against convention—"

"Oh, mother, you, of all people. What possible objection could anyone have to my marrying Cedric?"

"He's Jewish!"

* * *

Did you hear about the Jewish fag who died?

On his tombstone he had engraved:

GAY EN DRED

* * *

TELEPHONE RINGS

"Hello."

"Can I speak to Mrs. Levy, please?"

"Mrs. Levy isn't at home."

"Is Mr. Levy in?"

"No, sir, Mr. Levy is out."

"How about the children?"

"Nobody home but me."

"Who am I talking to?"

"This is Lena, the *Shvartzeh!*"

* * *

Bernbaum and Halperin, two *schnorrers,* were discussing Einstein's theory. "All it means is that everything is relative," Bernbaum explained. "It's like this, but it's also like that. It's entirely different, but it's the same thing. You understand?"

"No," Halperin said, "could you give me an example?"

"Of course. Let's say I screw you in the ass. I have a *putz* in the *tuchas*, and you have a *putz* in the *tuchas*. It's entirely different, but it's the same thing. Now you understand?"

"Ah-hah!" agreed the other, "but this is the way Einstein makes a living?"

* * *

How can you tell a Jewish baby in a nursery?

It's the one with heartburn.

* * *

Lou Custrini, M & M's California cracker-jack communications director came up with this cackler:

Meyer was staying at a Catskill resort hotel. After a few drinks too many, he staggered down to the lake and, seeing a rowboat, said to himself, "I think I'll take a row to Montreal!"

He jumped into the boat and began rowing. All night he rowed. But Meyer didn't know that a 100-foot rope tied the boat to the dock, preventing him from going any further than the center of the lake. He kept on rowing.

At four A.M. his distraught wife went down to the lake hoping to find her lost husband.

"Meyer!" she yelled. "Meyer!"

Meyer, still bombed and rowing furiously, murmured, "Who knows me in Montreal?"

* * *

Comedian Dave Barry tells about the black limousine that pulled up in front of a fancy Beverly Hills delicatessen.

An Arab got out, walked up to the deli counter and said, "I hear you got delicious sandwich here called pastrami."

Chislov, the counterman, stared at the Arab and said, "We got it, but for you it's $50."

"I'll take two," announced the Arab.

Chislov made the two sandwiches. The Arab laid down $100 and a $100 tip.

Next day, three black limousines pulled up in front of the deli, three Arabs got out and the spokesman said, "Yesterday, a friend of ours was in here and bought a delicious sandwich called pastrami. We would like the same."

"Okay," said Chislov, "but the price just went up to $100 a sandwich."

"We'll take six," said the spokesman.

Chislov fixed the six sandwiches, the Arab put down $600 and then gave Chislov a $1,000 tip.

The next day there was an unusually large sign in front of the deli:

NO JEWS ALLOWED

* * *

My Yiddishe Mama

From the third-floor window of a Brooklyn brownstone came the lilting sound of a Jewish mother:

"Sheldon, come down, do you hear? Come down or you'll break your legs. Sheldon, Mama's telling you! All right, Sheldon, but when you fall down and break both legs, don't come running to me!"

* * *

Lester was a very bright boy. One day he got a terrible tongue-lashing from his mother for using a four-letter word.

"But, Mama," he interrupted, "Tennessee Williams uses that word all the time."

"Well, don't play with him then!"

* * *

One hot summer day, Mrs. Saperstein took her little boy, Alan, to Jones Beach.

As soon as she settled under a beach umbrella, Mrs. Saperstein became a dutiful mother.

"Alan, Alan, come here! Don't run into the water. You'll get drowned!"

"Alan don't play with the sand. You'll get it in your eyes."

"Alan, Alan, don't stand in the sun. You'll get sunstroke."

"*Oy, vey!* Such a nervous child!"

* * *

When Mrs. Neidorf met Mrs. Silverstein at the supermarket, she noticed the look on her face. "You must be worried!" said Mrs. Neidorf.

"Listen," replied Mrs. Silverstein, "I have so many worries that if something happens today, I won't have time to worry about it for another two weeks."

* * *

Herbie walked into the house and said, "Ma, can I watch the solar eclipse?"

"Okay," she replied, "but don't go too close."

* * *

Nathan took his mother to Loew's Pitkin. The movie was about the hardships of an average family during the French Revolution. As they left the theatre Nathan said, "How'd you like it, Mama?"

"It was okay, but I don't understand. If they was so poor, how could they afford all that antique furniture?"

* * *

What is the plural of *yenta?*
Hadassah.

* * *

Genevieve Davis, the glamorous bestselling novelist, donated this delightful dilly:

Teenager Marvin got his first job delivering newspapers. At the end of the first week he received five one-dollar bills, which he gave to his mother.

At the end of the second week, he turned in only $4.97. By the third week, he came home with just $4.93. The fourth week, when Marvin again came in seven cents short, she sat down at the kitchen table.

"Now, Marvin," she said, "don't have no secrets from your mother. Tell me the truth, Sonny. Are you taking out a girl?"

* * *

How many Jewish mothers does it take to screw in a light bulb?

None. They'd rather sit in the dark.

* * *

Irene Ginsberg, Garden City's genial party giver, tells about Selma bumping into her next door neighbor, Mrs. Kreps. "Congratulate me," said Selma, "my daughter Shari just gave birth to a baby boy."

"How's that possible?" asked Mrs. Kreps. "She's only married five months."

"Listen," said Selma, "my Shari is such a young innocent girl, she knows how long to carry?"

* * *

The first ship on the Israeli sailing line to be launched was known as the *S.S. Mein Kindt*.

* * *

Mrs. Neiman, Mrs. Vogel and Mrs. Roth, three elderly widows, were sitting poolside at a Florida hotel drinking Mai Tais.

"I got such a rich son," said Mrs. Neiman, "his house in Montauk has 47 rooms and not one, but two, swimming pools built into the house."

"My son is a dentist," said Mrs. Vogel, "a doctor and a brain surgeon, and now just for fun he's graduating law school."

"My son," bragged Mrs. Roth, "has got some gorgeous body on him. That boy has a penis, twelve birds could stand in a row on it without even touching each other."

After a third round of drinks, Mrs. Neiman said, "Ladies, I gotta be honest. My son's fancy house, it's only nine rooms, and in the backyard there's just a wading pool for the children."

"To tell the truth," said Mrs. Vogel, "my son couldn't get into medical or law school. He just happens to have a couple of lawsuits on his hands."

"Girls," said Mrs. Roth, "as long we're being honest, I got a confession, too! The bird on the end of my son's *putz* has to stand on one leg!"

* * *

Ned Sukin, New Jersey's jocular spirits solicitor, savors this scintilla of silliness:

It was spring. The end of another school year. Yossel just graduated from an Orthodox rabbinical university. The bearded *yeshiva bucher* came home wearing his long black alpaca coat, skullcap, prayer shawl and ringlets.

As he entered the living room, his mother exclaimed, "Papa, look who's here. Joe College!"

* * *

During the Vietnam War, Leonard joined the Army. Now, he was on his way overseas. "Don't forget," said his mother, "when you get up in the morning you'll have a nice breakfast, then go out and kill a few Vietn*eese*. You'll come back, have a good lunch, not too much, then you'll go out and kill a few more."

"But, Mama," said the boy, "what if they should kill me?"

"Don't be silly," she replied, "what have they got against you?"

* * *

Sidney Miller, the famed TV and movie star, tells his friends about:

Little Arnold who had been hit by a car and was lying in the street. He had a concussion, ten crushed ribs, two broken arms and a fractured leg. Arnold's mother ran from the house to where the boy was lying. She knelt down beside him and whispered some comforting words in his ear. "Don't worry, Darling. When Mama gets you home I'm gonna give you a nice enema!"

* * *

Bill Jones, Carousel Caterers' convivial comic, came up with this cutie:

Mrs. Sussman walked into a butcher shop. "Where's the regular fella?" she asked.

"He's on vacation. I'm Manny. Can I help you?"

"Yeah. I want a nice Long Island duck."

Manny brought out a duck. Mrs. Sussman stuck two fingers up the fowl's rear end and shouted, "What're you tryin' to pull? That's a Wisconsin duck. I want Long Island."

The butcher came back in a minute with a replacement. Again Mrs. Sussman shoved two fingers up the duck's behind and exclaimed, "This is a Florida fowl. I want from Long Island."

Manny returned with a third duck. Once more Mrs. Sussman pulled her proctologist routine. "Now that's a Long Island duck!" she announced. "Wrap it up."

Upon leaving she said, "Say, how long you been working here?"

"Two weeks."

"Where you from?"

Manny bent over, aimed his butt at her an said, "You tell me!"

* * *

Mrs. Feinberg entered Altmans' Appetizer Store and asked for a pickled herring. Altman reached down into the herring barrel and pulled out a pickled herring—the last one in the store.

"Here's a nice herring. Shall I wrap it up?"

"It's nice, but I'm looking for a little bigger one."

Altman didn't want to lose the sale so he put the herring back in the barrel, then pulled it out again.

"Look, this one is perfect! Shall I wrap it?"

Mrs. Feinberg hadn't been shopping in appetizer stores for thirty years for nothing. "Listen," she said. "I changed my mind. I'll take both of them."

* * *

Mrs. Sonenberg telephoned a doctor from her expensive Miami Beach hotel room and complained of having chills. "Take your mink stole and wrap it around your feet, you'll feel better!" advised the doctor.

She called back 20 minutes later, "I'm still cold!"

"Take your sable stole," said the MD "wrap it around your shoulders and you'll be OK!"

* * *

A half hour later she called back.

"Doctor, I'm freezing to death!"

"Go to the closet, take your full length mink coat, get into it, then hop into bed and you'll be all right!"

The next day, Mrs. Sonenberg called the medical man and said, "You're certainly a wonderful doctor! But tell me, what do you do for your gentile patients?"

* * *

Esther Seidel, dynamic director of Little Neck's "Y," loves this lollapalooza:

Goldie met Rivka at Macy's. "I haven't seen you in a long time," said Goldie. "How's everything?"

"Don't ask," replied Rivka.

"What's the trouble?"

"Two weeks ago my husband dropped dead, a heart attack. Last Tuesday, my daughter was in an automobile accident and they had to cut off one leg and the other foot. Yesterday, my son left his wife and three children and ran away to live with another man. And tomorrow, the painters are coming!"

* * *

Sabina telephoned her house with some breathtaking news:

"Mama, I got married."

"Mazel tov!"

"I might as well tell you, he's not Jewish!"

"So he's a *goy!* I'm prejudiced?"

"But, Mama, he's also a Negro."

"All right, he's a *shvartzer*. By me everybody should be tolerant."

"Well, Mama, he's also out of work."

"Nu, so you'll support him. A wife she should help her husband."

"But, Mama, we have no place to live."

"Don't worry, darling. You'll stay right here in our house."

"But you only have one bedroom."

"That's all right. You and your new husband could sleep in the bedroom an Papa could sleep on the sofa in the living room."

"Yes, but Mama, where will you sleep?"

"Sabina dear, about me you got nothin' to worry. The minute I hang up, I'm gonna drop dead."

* * *

"My mother is a great housekeeper!" said Eli.

"Really?" said Harold.

"Yeah. In the middle of the night I get up to go to the bathroom, and when I come back the bed is made!"

* * *

40

Mrs. Orlowitz: My son's a homosexual.
Mrs. Lipshitz: That's nice. Where's his office?

*   *   *

Fay Krause, Rego Park's most noted National Council member, narrates this natural nip of nonsense:

Moish became an actor and after years of struggle finally hit it big in Hollywood. The studios fixed his nose and changed his name to Race Mallard.

Three years later he bought a penthouse overlooking Central Park and gave a great housewarming party. But Race Mallard was still Moish from Delancy Street and so he named his aged mother guest of honor. Everybody showed up but mama, and the actor was frantic with worry. Finally, he went to the lobby and said to the doorman, "Did you see a little old lady come in?"

"There was one," recalled the doorman. "She's been sitting over in that corner for about three hours now."

It was his mother. "Mama," he cried "Why didn't you come up to my apartment?"

"Tell you the truth," she said, "I couldn't remember your new name."

*   *   *

Mike Resner, New York's famous factoring administrator, gets guffaws with this flowery funny:

A Jewish gangster was dining at a kosher restaurant on New York's lower East Side when members of the mob came in and pumped him full of lead. He crawled out of the restaurant and stumbled up Rivington Street to the tenement of his childhood.

With hands clutching his bleeding stomach, he crawled up three flights of stairs and banged on the door of his mother's flat. He began sobbing, "Mama! Mama!"

His mother opened the door and discovered her only son lying in a puddle of blood. Again he wailed, "Mama! Oh, Mama!"

The old woman looked down at him and said, "*Bubeleh,* come in and eat—you'll talk later!"

* * *

After her husband passed on, Mrs. Altschul wanted to check into a posh Palm Beach hotel for a vacation. Friends warned her against it as the hotel was restricted.

Undismayed, Mrs. Altschul enrolled at an expensive speech school that would eliminate her thick Yiddish accent.

In three months Mrs. Altschul passed her diction course and headed for the restricted Florida hotel. The next morning at breakfast she sat with seven midwestern Waspish residents. In perfect clipped English she said, "Would you please pass the butter?"

As the man across from her passed the dish, Mrs. Altschul fumbled it and the butter landed on her dress. Whereupon she exclaimed, *"Oy vey!"* Then looking around, she added, "Whatever that means."

* * *

A young composer trying to write a hit song stayed at the piano in the attic despite his mother's pleas to eat. "Have some dinner, sonny?" she begged.

"Go away! I'm working!" he shouted.

The next morning the woman knocked at the door and cried, "How about a little breakfast?"

"Stop disturbing me," the boy screamed. "I'm trying to work."

The next day she pleaded, "Have a little lunch!"

* * *

"For the last time leave me alone!"

A week went by and the mother could stand it no longer. She prepared a tray of food and opened the attic door. The boy became hysterical. He grabbed the tiny woman and knocked her to the floor. Then he began pounding and beating her prostrate body. Suddenly he stopped, pulled her to his chest and shouted, "I've got it! I've got it!"

He rushed to the piano and began to play and sing, "My Yiddishe Mama. . . ."

* * *

Marital Mishmosh

Bornstein, the marriage broker, introduced his client Yonkel to the prospective bride. Yonkel was disappointed. "What are you doing?" he said to Bornstein, "making a fool out of me? Look at her! She's ugly and she's old. She squints. Look at those false teeth."

"Why are you whispering?" said the matchmaker. "She's deaf, too!"

* * *

The *shadchan* took a potential suitor to look at a possible bride. After a glance at her, he whispered to the broker: "Why is her ear on her neck? Why is one eye on top of the other? Why has she got only one nostril?"

"Obviously, you don't care for Picasso!" responded the broker.

* * *

Did you hear about the Jewish cowgirl who went for a cantor in the woods?

* * *

Minna, the matchmaker was building up the virtues of a particular girl. "She's beautiful, tall, well-built, a good cook, a smart woman, with integrity," she listed.

"Wait," said her client, "you left out one important thing!"

"What could I have left out?" said Minna.

"That she limps!" said the young man.

"Oh!" said the matchmaker. "But only when she walks!"

* * *

OVERHEARD AT CATSKILL RESORT

Rego Park
Jewish Prince: This may be a small diamond but it hasn't one rough flaw.

Rockville Center
Jewish Princess: In that diamond there's no room for a flaw.

* * *

Margolis told young Simon that he had the perfect girl for him. "She's a blonde!" he exclaimed with pride.

"You mean Tillie, the tailor's daughter?" cried Simon.

"That's the one," said the marriage broker.

"You're crazy! She's almost blind!"

"That's a blessing. Half the time she won't see what you're doing."

"But she also stutters."

"That's also a benefit. A woman that stutters will be afraid to speak. You'll live a peaceful life."

"But she's deaf!"

"I should have such luck! With a deaf wife you can shout, you can scream as much as you want to."

"But she's twenty years older than I am!"

"Ain't that something," exclaimed the matchmaker. "I bring you a woman with such gifts, and you pick on one little fault!"

* * *

JEWISH NYMPHOMANIAC

A girl who does it once a month

* * *

Nate's wife was a shrew. She never spoke to him in a normal voice; it was always a screech. One Friday he came home early and found his wife lighting the Sabbath candles and praying in a soft, melodious tone. Touched with her gentleness, he asked, "Rosalie, why don't you ever talk to me like you can talk to the candles?"

She answered, "If you would burn like the candles, I would talk to you the same way."

* * *

Irene and Norman had been quarreling for the twenty-five years of their married life. On their silver anniversary, she asked, "Well, how are we gonna celebrate?"

"How about two minutes of silence?" he suggested.

* * *

Robert Glazer, the Indianapolis real-estate impresario, rollicks clients with this rib-buster:

Sandra brought home Wilmot and introduced him as the boy she wanted to marry. "Is he Jewish?" asked her father.

"No, Dad," replied the girl.

"I will never permit my daughter to marry a *shaygets.*"

"I'm willing to be converted to Judaism," said Wilmot. "I'm in love with Sandra and I want to marry her."

"All right," said the father, "I agree."

So Wilmot got circumcised; went through the whole ritual but when the time came for the wedding, Sandra fell out of love with him. She didn't want to marry him!

Wilmot went to Sandra's father and said, "I agreed to become a Jew and I did. I've been circumcised and now your daughter won't marry me. What shall I do?"

"Easy," said the father. "Marry a *shiksa* like the other Jewish boys."

* * *

The Sheftels were sitting on the lawn of a posh Catskill resort enjoying themselves. "Listen to those little birds sing," said the wife. "They sound so happy!"

"Why shouldn't they be happy?" grumbled her husband. "It ain't costing them a hundred dollars a day!"

* * *

A Martian landed in Great Neck and saw Spivak watering his lawn. The man from outer space said, "Take me to your leader!"

"I can't," said Spivak, "she's in Monticello with the kids."

* * *

The Blumsteins were having an enormous argument. "OK, so I like to spend money," said the wife. "Name one other extravagance."

* * *

For their twentieth wedding anniversary, Shimsky bought his wife a family plot at the Hillside Memorial Park. As their twenty-first wedding anniversary approached, Mrs. Shimsky asked, "What are you going to give me this year for our anniversary?"

"Nothing," he replied. "You still didn't use what I gave you last year."

* * *

Herb and Irma decided to add a little culture to their lives. They went to the Metropolitan Museum of Art and took a guided tour of the exhibits.

"This is a fine bust of Michelangelo," said Herb.

"That's not Michelangelo," explained the guide. "That's Leonardo da Vinci."

Embarrassed by her husband's ignorance, Irma said, "Why do you have to open your big mouth when you don't know nothin' about the New Testament?"

* * *

One night, Fligelman, after a long, dry spell of no love-making began to move closer to his wife's side of the bed. Suddenly, she jumped up.

"Don't touch me, you sex fiend!" she screamed.

"Sweetheart," pleaded Fligelman, "once every six months doesn't make me a sex fiend!"

* * *

Rocklin, the millionaire clothing manufacturer, had an unmarried daughter, Reba, who looked like a witch. In order to find her a husband, Rocklin placed an ad in *Women's Wear Daily*.

Kleiner, a young salesman, showed up at the Rocklin home. When he saw how ugly Reba was he headed for the door. "Wait!" cried Rocklin, "with my daughter goes a big dowry."

"But she's so unattractive," moaned Kleiner.

"Listen," argued the father. "You'll get a mask that looks like that Bo Derek. Everytime you wanna make whoopie with the girl, you tell her to put on the mask. The dowry is $500,000."

They were married in the spring. Just before the honeymoon, Kleiner had a mask made that was the spitting image of Bo Derek. For the next five years he faithfully followed his father-in-law's advice. Before he made love to Reba he told her to put on the mask.

One afternoon, Reba was helping her husband hang a picture in their living room. Kleiner stood up on a ladder and suddenly dropped the nail. "Reba, hand me that nail?"

"Where is it?"

"Over there."

"Where?"

"To your right!" he pointed, getting slightly irritated.

"I can't find it!"

"For God's sake," shouted Kleiner, "it's right near your foot!"

"I don't see it!"

By then Kleiner had grown furiously frustrated and screamed, "Oh, go screw yourself!"

Reba said, "Should I get the mask?"

* * *

Fay Pavlove, the pleasing purveyor of Los Angeles United Book Service, offered this perky pinch of persiflage:

The Rosenthals were having breakfast.

"You don't talk nicely to me the way you used to," said Mrs. Rosenthal. "I suppose you just don't love me anymore."

"Don't love you!" growled the husband. "There you go again! Don't love you! Why, I love you more than life itself. Now shut up and let me read my newspaper."

* * *

"The new cleaning lady stole two of our towels, the crook!" exclaimed Mrs. Rivkin.

"Which towels, dear?" asked her husband.

"You know," she replied, "the ones we got from the hotel in Miami Beach."

Fannie was hanging up her husband Steve's jacket when she noticed a long gray hair on the shoulder.

"So," she screamed at him, "You've been over at your mother's getting sympathy again!"

* * *

JEWISH WIFE

A woman who is able to forgive and forget—except she'll never forget what she forgave.

* * *

The Pressmans were in bed. "Will you close the window?" said Mrs. Pressman. "It's cold outside."

Pressman paid no attention.

"Please close the window? It's cold outside."

No answer.

"This is the third time, I'm asking. Close the window! It's cold outside."

Pressman got up out of bed, slammed the window and said, "Okay, now it's warm outside?"

* * *

Ostrovsky came home from work and found his wife hysterical. "I was by the doctor today," she cried, "and he said I have tuberculosis and must die already."

"Impossible," shouted Ostrovsky. "You look too fat and healthy. I'll go see the doctor myself."

He rushed into the MD's office and said, "What's the idea telling my wife she has tuberculosis and must die?"

"I never told your wife that," said the doctor. "What I said was that she's got too big a *tuchis* and must go on a diet."

* * *

Milton was back from a six-month trip to Europe.

"Mom, Dad," he announced, "I want you to meet your new Norwegian daughter-in-law!" Milton spoke to the overweight blonde in her native tongue and she looked blank.

"This cow?" screamed his father. "This is what you bring home after all the money it cost to send you to Europe?"

"Dad," explained Milton, "she's no ordinary girl. Brunhilde is a baroness!"

"What!" roared his father. "You mean she can't even have children?"

* * *

Mrs. Greenbaum drove a beautiful new Cadillac to a used car lot and offered to sell it for $100. The dealer figured something had to be wrong with it. "I'm not sure I can use it," he said.

"Listen," said Mrs. Greenbaum. "The car is perfect. My husband died two weeks ago. He was having an affair with his secretary. And in his will he mentioned his secretary should have the proceeds from selling his new $20,000 Cadillac."

* * *

Bessie listened carefully as the doctor prescribed a remedy for her nervous condition. "You need frequent baths," he advised, "plenty of fresh air, and you should dresss in warm clothes."

That evening during dinner she told her husband about it. "The doctor," she announced "says I am in a highly nervous condition, that I gotta go to Miami, then a dude ranch out west and buy myself a full-length mink coat."

* * *

Hollywood producer, Chuck Stewart, tells of several men who were chatting at the Turkish baths about their honeymoons.

Friedlander couldn't remember the city where he spent his. "It's a place on the seashore what starts widda "T", he said.

The group racked their brains for an hour suggesting places but with no results. Finally they sent out for a map.

"There it is," shouted Friedlander. "*T*lentic City."

* * *

Nemzer persuaded the great pianist Arturo Rubinstein to listen to his daughter play the piano.

When she finished playing, the girl said, "What do you think I should do now?"

"Get married," said Rubinstein.

* * *

JEWISH FOREPLAY

Thirty Minutes of Begging

* * *

Ada and Lou decided to get a divorce. Since they couldn't agree on what to do about custody of their three children, Ada made this suggestion. "We'll stay together another year, have one more child and then get the divorce. That way we can divide the children, two for each person."

"But what if we have twins?" asked the husband.

"Hoo-hah! my twin-maker," scoffed the wife. "If I had to depend on you, would I have these three?"

* * *

Morey Amsterdam, the comic with the computer-mind, came up with this cutie while we were browsing at Doubleday's:

Bortnick and his wife were having breakfast. "Sweetheart," he said, "today is your birthday, go down to the furrier, get yourself a nice full-length sable. Spend $50,000, I don't care. Happy Birthday!"

"I don't want it!" said Mrs. Bortnick.

"All right. Go to the Rolls Royce people, get yourself a new car for seventy, eighty thousand, it's okay by me. Have a nice birthday!"

"I don't want it!"

"Sweetie pie. I want you should be happy. Go to Tiffany's. Pick out a tiara with diamonds, rubies, pearls, spend $150,000. Just have a happy birthday!"

"I don't want it!"

"For God's sake, whatta ya want?"

"A divorce!"

"Sweetness!" exclaimed Bortnick, "that I can't afford!"

* * *

Rabbinical Revelry

Mrs. Jacobson visited her rabbi with a number of domestic problems. For two hours, she unburdened her heart, recounting all the mean things her relatives were saying about her. Finally she got up to leave.

"Rabbi, when I came here I had a terrible headache," she smiled. "But now, thanks to you, it's gone."

"Mrs. Jacobson, your headache isn't gone at all," retorted the rabbi. "I have it!"

* * *

Rhoda, the rabbi's granddaughter returned from college for a visit. "Grandpa," said the liberated lady, "I'm really proud of you."

"What's to be proud?" asked the old man.

"I notice that when you sneeze you've learned to put your hand in front of your mouth."

"Of course," said the rabbi. "How else can I catch my teeth?"

* * *

It was a sweltering August Saturday. Inside the synagogue the rabbi droned endlessly—his voice a deadly monotone. The congregation fidgeted, squirmed in their seats and tried to stifle their yawns. A few tiptoed out of the temple. Others followed, one by one, until the entire audience had departed.

But the rabbi, oblivious to anything but his own voice, continued to preach. The sexton walked up to the rabbi and said, "Here's the key to the synagogue. Would you mind locking up when you're through?"

* * *

After Rosh Hashanah services, Mrs. Plotz, the old *yenta*, was leaving Beth Israel Synagogue when the rabbi stopped her.

"What did you steal there? Whatta ya got hidden under your dress?"

The old woman said, "Nothing!"

The rabbi grabbed and found that she had hidden a *siddur* there. At that moment, Mrs. Plotz let out a resounding fart.

The rabbi said, "My God, you also stole the *shofar!*"

Student: Rabbi, why did God make man before woman?

Rabbi: Because He didn't want any advice on how to make man!

* * *

Kaminsky left Pinsk to work in Minsk. For six months he had been away and was very anxious to get back home to his wife and children. It was late Friday afternoon, and his friend Malovich said, "It's against our religion to travel on the Sabbath. Stay with me until it's over."

"No," said Kaminsky. "I wanna get back to Pinsk. Six months I've been away."

"So what's another day? Stay with me. I've got a nice house. I'll give you good Jewish meals."

Kaminsky finally gave in and remained over the Sabbath. Even then Malovich would not let him go and insisted on his staying yet another day. Finally, Kaminsky said, "I can't stay another minute. I'm going home right now."

"All right," said Malovich, and he handed him a bill for food and lodging.

"What? You make me stay when I don't want to. You insist I be your guest. Then you give me a bill! I won't pay it."

"All right. We'll consult the rabbi."

The rabbi heard the whole story, stroked his beard, and pored at length over his law books. At last, he delivered his verdict: "You must pay."

Anxious to get home to Pinsk, Kaminsky paid the money and demanded a receipt. His friend took the money, receipted the bill, and then handed the money back again, saying, "Forget it!"

"Are you nuts?" screamed Kaminsky. "You force me to be your guest; you give me a bill; you drag me to the rabbi; he tells me I gotta pay; I pay; and now you give me back the money. What is this?"

"Ah," said Malovich, "I just wanted you to see what kind of a dope we got for a rabbi in Minsk."

* * *

The great rabbi lay dying. Devoted students flocked to his home to offer their respects. The visitors stood at his bedside murmuring high praise.

"So pious!" mourned one man.

"So learned!" grieved another.

"So charitable!" said a third.

The rabbi listened quietly. Then suddenly he raised himself up and said, "Piety! Learning! Charity! Fine! And about my great modesty you have nothing to say?"

* * *

When Mishkin died no one really cared. He was not a well-liked man. But his wife pleaded with the rabbi to deliver the eulogy. "I know he was a terrible person, but certainly you could find something nice to say about him."

The rabbi agreed.

Next day in the funeral parlor the rabbi spoke: "Here lies Irvin Mishkin. Nice he wasn't. He beat his wife. He drank. He ran around with *shiksas*. He never gave to charity. He was a real louse, but compared to his brother, Ira, he was an *angel!*"

* * *

Baumgarten could not marry off his ugly daughter. He went to see Rabbi Pearlman of Pinsk for counsel. "My heart is heavy because God has given me an ugly daughter."

"How ugly?" asked the rabbi.

"If she were lying on a plate with a herring you wouldn't be able to tell the difference."

"What kind of herring?" asked Rabbi Pearlman.

"Er—Bismarck," replied the forlorn father.

"Too bad," said the rabbi. "If it was Maatjes, she'd have a better chance."

* * *

Noriko Stern, Florida's most beautiful Japanese Jew, gets giggles with this jolly jest:

A brilliant Hasidic rabbi from Brooklyn was invited to speak in Montgomery, Alabama, at a Southern Hadassah convention. He was dressed in typical rabbinical attire: wide-brimmed hat, beard, sideburns and long black coat.

When the Brooklyn rabbi got off the train, a group of southerners standing near the station began to laugh and make fun of him. He walked over to them and said, "Whatsa matter, you never saw a Yankee before?"

* * *

Old man Moskowitz, a very religious orthodox Jew, had been wearing the same prayer shawl to the synagogue for years. It became shabby and worn. One day he walked in wearing a brand-new one.

"Where did you get the nice new *tallis?*" asked the rabbi.

"My son-in-law gave it to me for Christmas!" replied Moskowitz.

* * *

Salick asked the rabbi to give his son some private Hebrew lessons. After several months of tutoring, the only Hebrew the boy had mastered were the first few words of the *Kaddish*, the prayer said for a departed parent.

"I wanted you to teach him some Hebrew," said Salick, "but why the prayer for the dead? I'm only thirty-four. You think I'm gonna die any minute?"

"Mr. Salick," explained the rabbi, "you should live so long as it'll take your son to learn the *Kaddish*."

* * *

For the first vacation in his whole life, Finkelstein flew to China. One evening while strolling through the outskirts of Shanghai, he heard the sound of chanting.

He followed the sound and discovered that it came from a building hidden behind some trees. A sign outside, in Chinese, read, "B'nai Wong Synagogue."

Finkelstein looked inside and found a service in progress. There was a cantor, rabbi, men in skullcaps, shawls, dark suits, women sitting in the balcony. The whole scene was Jewish except all of the people at the service were Chinese.

When the service was over, Finkelstein stopped the rabbi. "Could you tell me what religion you are?"

"I'm Jewish," replied the rabbi in Chinese. "We're all Jewish. And we have been holding a service."

"But you're all Chinese," said the traveler.

"That's right," said the rabbi.

"Look at me," said Finkelstein. "I'm Jewish."

"Funny," said the rabbi, "you don't look Jewish!"

* * *

Jonas and Schloss were talking about their synagogue. "Rabbis have a pretty easy life," said Jonas. "They pray, they preach, and they make good money for that. Besides, comes a wedding or funeral, they pick up a nice little fee!"

"Well," replied Schloss, "like my father used to say. The rabbi gets the fees, but it's the *mohel* who gets the tips!"

* * *

Did you hear about the rabbi who doubled as a press agent?

He saved his own clippings.

* * *

Fenster had trouble with his watch so he went to a jewelry store. "Would you please repair my watch!" he said.

The man behind the counter said, "I'm sorry I can't. I'm a *mohel!*"

"What do you mean? This is a watch store. You got watches hanging in the window."

"I'm a *mohel!* What could I hang in the window!"

* * *

Molly stood in the women's balcony in the synagogue on Yom Kippur. Reciting a long list of her sins, she beat herself on the crotch instead of the breast.

"Hey," said her friend Sonia, "you're not supposed to hit yourself there; you're supposed to hit yourself here!"

"Leave me alone, I'm hitting myself where I sin the most."

* * *

Paul Saltzman, New York's prominent CPA, tells about a truly religious man named Jacobs. He obeyed the Sabbath, not riding, smoking or handling money. One Saturday, while vacationing at a Catskill resort, he put on his red sport jacket and decided to walk through the fields.

A bull, seeing the red jacket, ran after him. In seconds it impaled Jacobs on his horns and was running wild with him. Jacobs waved his arms and screamed hysterically. Another hiker heard him and yelled, "What's the matter, Jacobs?"

"I'm riding on *Shabbes!* Help! Help!"

* * *

A wealthy cloak-and-suiter who lived in Scarsdale with his wife and children also kept one of his models in a fancy apartment on Riverside Drive. Occasionally he would visit Las Vegas to gamble, and he frequently imbibed more freely than was good for him.

One day the rabbi came to see him for a donation to a charity.

"I'm sorry," said the cloak-and-suiter, "but I already gave. You see, I always donate secretly."

"Isn't it strange," said the rabbi, "you can sin in secret and all of New York knows about it, but not a living soul ever hears about the charity you give secretly?"

* * *

Old man Halpern realized that death was not too far in the future. He decided to get on the good side of God. So he went to the rabbi and asked that he once again be part of the congregation.

The rabbi asked, "Are you going to repay all your debts and forgive those who are indebted to you?"

"Just a minute," protested Halpern, "you ain't talking religion now—you're talking business!"

* * *

The Edelmans moved from Brooklyn into a new senior citizen condominium complex in Florida. Edelman called the manager immediately and complained.

"Listen, my door is made from aluminum. I can't hang up a *mezuzah!*"

"Don't worry about it," said the manager, "we have a master *mezuzah* on the roof . . . You just plug into it!"

* * *

Bostwick hated all Jews. He didn't know why. He spent his entire life loathing God's chosen people and at the same time trying to find out about them.

One night, the anti-semite tiptoed to the doorway of a Jewish house, ripped off the *mezuzah* and ran. At last he was going to discover the secrets of the Jews!

Fearing he was being followed, Bostwick rushed home and locked the door. He got a knife and broke open the *mezuzah*. Inside was a piece of parchment. With trembling hands Bostwick unrolled the paper. On it was written: "Help! I'm a prisoner in a *mezuzah* factory."

* * *

Warren Cowan, America's premier show biz publicist, points up this playful pleasantry:

Moses stood on the shore of the Red Sea, gazed upon the vast expanse of ocean that barred the avenue of escape for his people. Not far behind, the Egyptians were in hot pursuit of the fleeing Israelites.

Moses turned to his public relations man. "Say," he exclaimed. "Suppose I were to raise my left hand and immediately the waters of the Red Sea parted and allowed us to pass through. And then suppose that after our people had crossed over safely to the other side, I raised my right hand and closed the parted waters, drowning the Egyptian soldiers who are chasing us!"

"Listen, Moe," said the PR man, "you pull off a miracle like that and I'll guarantee you ten whole pages in the Bible!"

* * *

Selma Solomon, the XL Stationers' super saleslady, loves this looney bit of levity:

Mrs. Janowitz was having tea with the rabbi's wife. "Did you notice Mrs. Garfinkel's hair at Friday evening services?" asked Mrs. Janowitz. "I could swear she had it dyed."

"I really didn't notice," said the rabbi's spouse.

"And the nerve of that Mrs. Zimmer coming to temple with a strange man. Her poor husband hasn't even been dead a year!"

"Frankly, I didn't notice that either."

"Well, did you notice that Rifka Cahn? Just because a girl is in college, does it mean she should wear a dress above her knees to synagogue? What do you think of that?"

"I'm afraid I didn't see that either."

"For heaven's sake!" snapped Mrs. Janowitz. "What good does it do you to be a rabbi's wife?"

* * *

The rabbi's wife went to the *mikveh* on Friday afternoon. There was a long line so she asked the last lady in line, "Can I go ahead of you? The rabbi is waiting for me."

And so she went along the whole line. Finally she got to the first woman waiting and asked, "Can I go ahead of you? I'm the rabbi's wife and he's waiting for me."

"No, you can't go ahead of me. I'm the town whore and for me the whole town is waiting!"

* * *

Bertha Mae, a young black girl, left Alabama and after only a week in New York landed a job in the Hymowitz household. A year later she returned home and her mother asked, "How you like working for those Jewish people?"

"Well, they is real funny, Mama. They has a holiday they call *Shabbes* where they eat in the dining room and smoke in the bathroom.

"Then they's got one called *Tisha Bov*. That's when they smoke in the dining room and eat in the bathroom.

"Then they got another one they calls *Yom Kippur*. That's when they eat *and* smoke in the bathroom!"

* * *

The butler of a wealthy Beverly Hills family was chatting with the Mexican maid.

"Working for a Jewish family is very interesting," he said. "They have all sorts of curious customs. For instance, during one holiday, before they sit down to dinner the head of the family blows the *shofar*."

"Say," said the maid, "they sure do know how to treat the help!"

* * *

Rickey and Lamar, two black shoeshine boys, were standing near a synagogue.

Rickey: How come you make all the money 'round here?

Lamar: It's easy, when Mr. Edelson comes out of the synagogue I say, "Good *Shabbes,* Mr. Edelson," or I say, "Good *Yontif,* Mr. Bortnick, how was the service today?"

Rickey: But how you remember all these things?

Lamar: It's nothing (pointing to his head). I keep 'em right up here in my *tuchis!*"

* * *

Novacoff rushed to the synagogue on Rosh Hashanah and was stopped at the entrance. "Where's your ticket?" asked the doorman.

"I ain't got one!"

"You ain't got a ticket, you can't get in!"

"Look, I'm not going to pray. I just wanna tell Spiegel his store is on fire."

"Well," said the doorman, "that's a different story. Go ahead in. But if I catch you *davening* I'll break your arm!"

* * *

Kronfeld had been a devout Orthodox Jew, but in the latter part of his life he turned to Catholicism.

His parish priests were ecstatic. This would be wonderful propaganda for the universal appeal of the church, and so they invited him to speak at the next theological seminar.

Kronfeld got up, looked around the room, and said, "Fellow *goyim*. . . ."

* * *

Tony Noice, Sitmar's consummate cruise director, pleases passengers with this pearl:

Morris Lefkowitz knelt at the altar of Calvary Lutheran Church.

"In the name of the Father, the Son and the Holy Ghost, I now baptize you and welcome you into the Kingdom of Christ," intoned the minister, sprinkling the new convert with water.

Lefkowitz arose and the preacher shook his hand. "Now that you have been baptized you may choose a Christian name if you wish," he said. "Have you given it any thought?"

"Yes, Reverend," answered Lefkowitz. "I would like to be called Martin Luther."

"Well," beamed the minister, "you certainly have chosen a famous Christian name. May I ask the reason?"

"You see," explained the ex-Morris Lefkowitz, "I don't wanna change the initials on my laundry."

* * *

"The trouble with you Jews," said Father Sullivan to Rabbi Bender, "is that your people are too old fashioned and set in your ways. What you should do is catch up with the modern world—go in for public relations and advertising."

"My dear friend, you don't know anything about ancient Jewish history or you wouldn't say that," replied the rabbi. "Our mighty Samson had the idea for advertising more than three thousand years ago. He took two columns and brought down the house!"

* * *

Father Fogarty and Rabbi Shenberg were seated opposite each other at a banquet where some delicious roast ham was served. "This is absolutely scrumptious," remarked the priest.

Presently, he leaned forward and said to the Orthodox clergyman, "Rabbi Shenberg, when are you going to become liberal enough to eat ham?"

"At your wedding, Father Fogarty," retorted the rabbi.

* * *

"The Pope is the one with the *yarmulkah!*"

Braverman commuted every day from Great Neck to New York. One morning while waiting for the Long Island train, he spotted his friend Cantrowitz crossing himself. "Hey, since when did you convert?" he asked.

"Whatta ya talkin' about?" replied Cantrowitz.

"I just saw you crossing yourself."

"Don't be ridiculous," said his friend. "I was just checking—hat, zipper, fountain pen, wallet."

* * *

Zeitlin and Rosenbaum were passing a store that sold religious items. In the window were pictures of Mary in the manger, Mary holding Christ in the manger, Mary and Joseph and Christ in the manger.

"What is all that?" asked Zeitlin.

"Those are paintings depicting Christ in the manger," explained Rosenbaum.

"That's how *goyim* are," said Zeitlin. "They can't afford to go to a hotel but they spend money to have their pictures taken!"

* * *

Rabbis Engel and Stern went to the Marcus Pincus Clothing Store and picked out new suits. "Are these suits black," asked Rabbi Engel, "or are they dark blue?"

"Black!" said Pincus. "These suits are black—perfect for a rabbi—no blue at all!"

They bought the suits and started walking uptown. On the way, Rabbi Stern said, "I wonder if the suits are really black."

At that moment two nuns, Sisters Eunice and Mary Elizabeth, were approaching.

"Nuns wear pure black," said Rabbi Engel. "Let's compare the color of the suits with the nuns' habits." Rabbi Stern stopped Sister Eunice and said, "Sister, what time is it?"

As she looked at her wristwatch, he quickly placed the coat next to her shoulder to make a comparison.

When the nuns reached their convent they went to the Mother Superior. "We met two men today who looked like Jews but who spoke Latin," said Sister Eunice.

"Latin!" exclaimed the Mother Superior. "How do Jews come to speak Latin?"

"Well," said Sister Mary Elizabeth, "I heard it clear as crystal. One of them exclaimed 'Marcus pincus fuctus!' "

* * *

Alter Kockerim

Octogenarian Kornblum lay dying. His wife sat by his bedside. A terrible snowstorm had begun. The flakes fell so fast and furiously that visibility was zero.

"I'm about to die," said Kornblum. "Send for a priest."

"Not only you're dying, you're also losing your mind," said his wife. "Don't you mean a rabbi?"

Kornblum said, "You want a rabbi should go out on a night like this?"

* * *

Littner, aged 78, was struck down by a car. As he lay in the street, Father Flynn from a neighborhood church was quickly summoned to comfort the old man.

The priest kneeled down beside him and asked, "Do you believe in the Father, the Son, and the Holy Ghost?"

The old man moaned, "Here I am dying, and you're asking me riddles!"

Did you hear about the *zayde* of 92 who married a woman of 84?

They spent the whole honeymoon getting out of the car.

* * *

Rubin developed a rare disease and the doctor told him that the only cure would be castration. Rubin became hysterical while the doctor looked at him in amazement since he knew Rubin was in his eighties.

"Why should you feel so upset," asked the MD. "You don't even need them anymore."

"Yeah," Rubin answered, "but they look so sporty in the steam room."

* * *

Beverly Aucoin, show biz exec sec, got this giggler from attorney husband, Joe:

In a Florida retirement city, Mrs. Sachs, 78, brought Goldfarb her former boyfriend into court, claiming he'd stolen her furniture.

"I didn't do it!" cried the defendant. "She gave me that junk, and money, too."

"Why would she do that?" asked the white-haired judge.

"For sex," replied the old fellow. "What else?"

"Don't listen, Your Honor!" shouted Mrs. Sachs. "He's even older than you are. He must be taking pills to say such crazy things!"

* * *

Grandpa Schwartzwald lay in bed very close to death. His children and grandchildren stood in the living room waiting for the end. Stanley, the youngest grandson, peeked into the bedroom for a last look at the old man. Schwartzwald beckoned to the boy.

"What's that smell from the kitchen?" asked the dying man.

"Grandma is making sponge cake," replied the youngster.

"Go ask her if I could have just a little piece," said the dying man.

The boy returned in a moment and announced, "Grandma says you can't have any. It's for later!"

* * *

Old man Schlossberg brought a package to the post office, but the clerk refused to accept it.

"What's the matter?"

"It's too heavy. You'll have to put more stamps on it."

"And if I put more stamps on it, that'll make it lighter?"

* * *

Fritzi Burr, the brilliant Broadway and television actress, broke up a Hollywood synagogue crowd with this beaut:

Ike moved into a Miami Beach Senior Citizens' hotel and on the second night noticed Sarah sitting in the lobby. They struck up a conversation and soon began meeting for chit-chat.

One night Ike said, "You're such a nice person, could I take you to dinner?"

"Why not?" she replied. "The only thing is I'm a liberated woman. I don't let a man pay for me for nothing. I have to buy my own dinner."

"All right, so go get your pocketbook."

For the next seven days Ike and Sarah ate breakfast, lunch and dinner together. Never once did Sarah allow her escort to pick up the check. The senior citizens became so enamored of each other after a week they wound up in Sarah's room.

After a beautiful evening of lovemaking, Ike got dressed and was about to leave. "Sweetie," said Sarah, "before you go, put a $100 on the dresser."

"What!" screamed Ike. "The whole week we went out, you wouldn't let me spend a dime, now you want a hundred dollars!"

"You don't understand, darling!" she begged. "This I do for Hadassah!"

* * *

Audrey Wildman, the nifty New Jersey personal shopper, narrated this naughty nugget:

Hyman, 83, met Golda, 78, at a Miami Beach Senior Citizen Dance. It was love at first sight and, just as importantly, they agreed that two could live better on two social security checks.

Three days later, Hyman and Golda were married. That night they consummated the marriage with a long and lusty bout of lovemaking. When it was over Golda noticed that Hyman didn't move. She looked more closely and realized her worst fears. Hyman was dead. He had died just as he concluded the sex act.

At the funeral, Golda was approached by a friend, "I'm so sorry," she said, "what happened?"

"Nothing!" replied Golda. "He came and he went!"

* * *

Isadore and Gussie, both in their seventies got married and checked into the Holiday Inn right after the ceremony.

They undressed and climbed into bed. Suddenly, the old man got up, went to the bathroom and returned wearing a condom. "Listen," exclaimed the woman, "you can't give me a baby and I'm too old to get pregnant. So what are you wearing that rubber for?"

"Well," said the old man, "I got arthritis and the doctor told me not to go in damp places!"

* * *

Bassman, age 60, and Weinstock, 81, were sitting on a park bench. "I don't know," said Bassman. "I just can't seem to satisfy my wife. I try—but nothing."

"I don't have no problem," said Weinstock, the octogenarian. "Every night I come home, I get undressed in front of my wife, and I say, 'Take a look. Are you satisfied?' She shrugs, 'Yes,' and that's it."

* * *

Warburg, Lewisohn and Feinstein, three retired millionaires, were sunning themselves at the Fountainbleau. "Now that we can afford it, it's hard to enjoy," said Warburg. "Here I am in this beautiful place with all these gorgeous women around and my eyesight is so bad I can hardly make out the surroundings."

"It's my stomach that's killing me," said Lewisohn. "I could afford lobster, but I gotta eat spinach. I love champagne, but I have to drink milk."

"I got a problem, too," said Feinstein, "just last night I asked my wife to roll over and she said, 'What! Not again. We just finished the third one fifteen minutes ago.' You see, with me it's memory."

* * *

Feingold was visiting his aged father at the Sholom Retirement Home.

"There is one advantage to old age."

"What's that, Poppa?" asked Feingold.

"I can sing and brush my teeth at the same time."

* * *

Jackie Kahane, the Canadian comic who appeared for years on the bill with Elvis Presley, talks about his ethnic background:

"I'm from Canada but I come from an Orthodox neighborhood. Of course, you weren't really Orthodox unless you drank tea from a *yortzeit* glass.

"My aunt was so Orthodox she drank from the glass with the candle still in it!"

* * *

Here's another of Jackie's gems:

"When I arrived in New York I knew it was going to be tough for me to find work because everybody in that city is a comedian. I was down in the subway and I said to this little old man, 'Why do they call this the Independent Subway?'

"He said, 'Cause it comes when it wants to!' "

* * *

Al Bernie, the clever comedian/television writer, gets belly laughs with this bit of banter:

Rosenberg retired, and just to keep busy he taught his dog, Poopy, how to pray. Mrs. Rosenberg was so proud she made the canine a *tallis* and a *yarmulkah* and Rosenberg took Poopy to temple for the High Holidays.

When the congregation rose, Poopy stood up, and he howled as the people prayed. Sokol, another elderly man, was praying next to the dog. He looked at Poopy and the dog howled louder.

Sokol said to Rosenberg, "Is that your dog?"

"Yeah, it's mine."

"This dog is *davening!*" said Sokol.

"So?"

"It's none of my business," said Sokol, "but this dog should be on television."

"You tell him," said Rosenberg. "He wants to be an accountant."

* * *

A blind Black man stood on the corner of 54th Street and Fifth Avenue tapping his white cane in the hope someone would lead him across. Finally, gray-haired Mrs. Shoenberg took the Black by the arm and led him to the opposite side of the street.

"Thank you," said the Black.

"You're welcome," replied Mrs. Shoenberg. "It ain't easy to be blind."

"Yes, ma'am."

"How long you been like this?"

"I've been blind ever since I was a baby."

"My God!" said Mrs. Shoenberg. "You mean you don't even know that you're a *shvartzer?*"

* * *

Melinda Corey, the lovely Chicago literary rep, brightens up faces with this lighthearted lampoon:

Berel and Riva took the Hadassah bus tour to Mount Vernon, George Washington's beautiful home on the Potomac. They were enthusiastically admiring the various rooms. "And did you notice," said Berel, "everything is furnished Early American?"

* * *

"What's your new sister look like?" asked little Emma of her playmate.

"The baby's got Mama's eyes and Daddy's nose, and if Grandpa doesn't take his face out of the crib she's going to have his teeth!"

* * *

Mrs. Greenfield, a heavily bejeweled Long Island widow, sat in the office of a leading plastic surgeon.

"What will the operation of lifting my face cost?" she asked.

"Five thousand dollars," replied the doctor.

"That's too much," she protested. "Isn't there something less expensive?"

"You might trying wearing a veil," he answered.

* * *

A New England insurance company discovered that people on the lower East Side of New York live longer than they do elsewhere in the nation. So they sent Maclain, an actuary expert, down to talk to the residents.

The insurance man found Friedman, 97, and asked him several questions. Finally, Maclain said to him, "Since you've lived here all these years, what would you say the death rate is in this community?"

"Well," said the old man, "I would say it's about one to a person."

* * *

Bob Shortal, RCA's radiant East Coast news and info director, gets roars with this riotous rib-tickler:

Bubba Mendelbaum was approaching her ninetieth birthday. The children, grandchildren and great grandchildren prepared for a gala celebration. "Mama," asked her oldest son, "what would you like for a present? Just name it! You can have anything you want!"

"Just wanna sit!" replied the old woman.

"How about a ride in an airplane?" suggested another son. "I could arrange the flight."

"I ain't ridin' in no new flyin' machine," said the old lady. "I'll just sit here and watch television, like God intended I should."

* * *

Professor Marvin Levine, the erudite educator cracks up classes with this chuckler:

Old Rifkin complained of severe pains in his left leg. His doctor tried various treatments and medication but the pain persisted.

The old man was becoming impatient. "There must be something you can do for the pain in my leg!"

"Sit down, Mr. Rifkin," said the MD. "Even doctors have their limitations. You understand that, with advancing age, certain deterioration takes place. Try to remember that your leg is eighty-four years old!"

"Okay," said the old man. "But tell me something, is my other leg maybe ten years younger?"

* * *

"Just how old are you, Mister?" asked the judge.

"Eighty-nine!" answered Goldfarb, "and still plugging away!"

"Don't listen!" yelled Mrs. Sachs. "He's on pills. . . ."

"Please be silent, Madam!" demanded the elderly judge. "I'm trying to find out what kind of pills he's on!"

* * *

JEWISH EX-LAX

Let My People Go

Milt Fields, the munificent Miami show biz impresario, gets howls from this merry mirthful:

Old man Rosenbloom opened his eyes and discovered a woman in a white uniform staring at him. "Where am I?" he asked.

"You were in an auto accident and you've been unconscious for six days!" replied the nurse. "You're in the best hospital with the best doctors, getting the finest medical care."

"I'm here six days?" asked the senior citizen. "No wonder I'm hungry. Could you bring me a corned beef sandwich?"

"No, you're being fed rectally," said the woman. "See those tubes? If you reach under and behind you you'll feel a large tube stuck up in you!"

"If this is the best hospital, with the best doctors, and I'm getting the finest medical care, you must have more tubes."

"Yes, Mr. Rosenbloom, we have plenty of tubes. Why do you ask?"

"Tomorrow, bring two more tubes, I'd like you and the doctor to join me for lunch!"

* * *

The Whole World is Jewish

In Israel during the period of a sniping on the Jaffa seafront, Yakov saw a dejected-looking friend standing by a wall. "What's wrong, Chaim?" he asked.

"Everything," replied the other. "My wife's left; my son's been arrested for stealing; my daughter's eloped; my bookkeeper's absconded; and I'm going bankrupt. I'm gonna throw myself into the sea."

"Then what are you waiting for?" asked Yakov. "It's only fifty yards away."

"How can I cross the square when the Arabs are sniping? I might get killed!"

* * *

Israel has just come up with a new car called a Bagel. It doesn't run on gasoline—it uses seltzer.

And when you press on the horn, it says, *"Gay avek! Gay avek!*

* * *

In the maternity ward of a hospital in Tel Aviv, Leah, a student nurse, walked from bed to bed, asking questions and making notations on her chart.

"Good morning!" she said to a pale-looking patient. "I understand your baby was born during the night. *Mazel tov!* Have you decided on a name for the baby for we'd like to record it?"

"Yes . . . I want to call him Arafat!"

"Arafat? Are you serious?" asked Leah.

"Of course."

"You are free to name him whatever you want. But are you sure, Mrs. Steinberg, that's the name you wish!"

"Yes, I'm sure! And, by the way, nurse, it's Miss Steinberg, not Mrs. Steinberg."

* * *

Ben Canaan sat down in a train between two Arabs. He nodded in a friendly manner, but the Arabs sat in stony silence. The Israeli noticed an Egyptian newspaper on the opposite seat and picked it up to read.

In a few minutes he turned to the Arab on his right and said, "You look like an intelligent man. I cannot quite make out this word. Would you be good enough to tell me what it is?"

The Arab winked to the other Arab and said, "The word is 'syphilis'!"

Ben Canaan thanked him and read on. A few minutes later, he was again stumped by a word. Turning to the other Arab, he said, "You are ob-

* * *

viously a man of education. Would you kindly tell me what this word is?"

The Arab winked at the other Arab and replied, "The word is 'gonorrhea'!"

"Syphilis *and* gonorrhea!" said the Israeli. "Oh that poor Yasir Arafat!"

* * *

What is Zionism?
When one Jew instructs another to collect money from a third to send a fourth to Palestine.

* * *

A Jew was forced to flee his old homeland and go to Israel.

"Dear God," he sighed, "two thousand years we pray in vain to return—and now it has to happen to me!"

* * *

The tower bell at the Vatican stopped working. Repairmen were brought in from all parts of the world to fix the bell, but they failed. After months of searching, an Israeli repairman was found and he agreed to fly to Italy and fix the bell for a nominal fee.

After months of silence, all of Rome was informed that the bell was fixed and would peal once again at 6:00 A.M. on Sunday.

One hundred thousand people gathered. A hush fell over the city as the hour approached, and then the bell began to peal, *"Goyim-m-m! Goyim-m-m! Goyim-m-m!"*

* * *

The Israeli army had been organized hastily and so promotions were quick. Lieutenant Landau suddenly found himself elevated to Major. He had been in his new office only a few minutes when someone knocked on the door.

The new Major, wanting to impress the caller, said, "Come in!" Then he picked up the phone on his desk and pretended to have an important discussion. "Yes, Mr. Ben-Gurion, I agree, but perhaps you should reserve your decision until I have had time to think about it. Thank you, Mr. Ben-Gurion, and I'll expect you and the missus at my house this evening for dinner."

Major Landau hung up the receiver and turned to the visitor. "All right, young man," he said, "what can I do for you?"

"Nothing sir," replied the stranger. "I'm here to install your telephone."

* * *

"Did you hear a group of Syrians robbed the Bank of Israel?"

"Really?"

"Yeah, they got away with 10 million dollars' worth of pledges."

* * *

Gitterman, an Odessa merchant drove his horse and loaded wagon to a neighboring town. A customer stopped him and asked, "What are you selling today?"

Gitterman whispered in his ear, "Oats."

"Why the secrecy?" demanded the customer.

"S-s-sh," said the merchant. "Not so loud, I don't want the horse to hear."

* * *

Ahmad and Abdul, two Arab prisoners of the Six Day War, were discussing their defeat.

"Why do you think we did so badly?" asked Ahmad. "Was it because the Russian weapons were no good?"

"The weapons were fine," said Abdul. "It was the Russian military textbooks that let us down."

"What did they say?"

" 'First retreat and draw the enemy into your own territory. Then wait for the winter snows. . . .' "

* * *

During a battle in the Crimean War a Russian officer addressed his troops. "The time has come! We are going to charge the enemy. It will be man against man in hand-to-hand combat!"

"Excuse me, Lieutenant," said Katchkin, the only Jewish soldier in the company. "Could you show me my man? Maybe I can come to an understanding with him!"

* * *

Private Kuhn was drafted into the Tsar's army. He arrived at the front, climbed down into a trench and asked:

"Excuse me, gentlemen, could you tell me which way are the prisoners-of-war?"

* * *

Koratsky and a Cossack were in court. Koratsky accused the Cossack of stealing his horse.

"I didn't steal it," protested the Russian soldier, "I found it."

"Liar!" screamed Koratsky. "What do you mean, you 'found' it? I was on the horse at the time. You forced me off with your whip!"

"Was the Jew on his horse?" asked the judge.

"Well, I found both of them, but I had no use for the Jew."

* * *

Gene Somach, City of Hope's fabulous fund raiser, features this fossil of frivolity:

Mashefsky, driving a small cart drawn by a donkey came to a toll bridge.

"You gotta pay a toll before you can go across!" said the Tsarist toll collector.

"What!"

"Yes, five kopecks to go over this bridge."

After an argument Mashefsky paid the five kopecks and went on. In the afternoon he came back again, but this time he had the donkey sitting on the seat and Mashefsky was dragging the cart himself.

"Hold it!" said the toll man. "You know you gotta pay five kopecks."

Mashefsky pointed to the donkey and said: "Don't talk to me! Ask the driver."

* * *

FRENCH INDIANS

Tresbientas

* * *

Broadway theatrical rep, Ken Grayson tells about the SS Major in charge of a concentration camp. He called over prisoner Edberg.

"Come here, Jew! Listen to me. I've got a glass eye. If you guess which one it is nothing will happen to you. If you guess wrong, I'll shoot you on the spot. Which one is it?"

"The left one, Herr Kommandant."

"How the hell did you guess?"

"It's got such a kind look about it."

* * *

Three alleged Trotskyists, a Pole, a Czech and a Jew were sentenced to death. Before being shot each was granted a last wish.

"I want my ashes scattered over the grave of Pilsudski," said the Pole.

The Czech said, "I want my ashes scattered over the tomb of Masaryk."

The Jew said, "I want my ashes scattered over the tomb of Comrade Kosygin."

"But that's impossible! Kosygin's not dead yet!"

"I know," said the Jew. "But I can wait!"

* * *

A KGB agent knocked at the door of a shabby Moscow apartment. On the door was a plate with the name *Shoenfeld* on it. An old man in a shabby, tattered coat opened the door.

"Yes?"

"Does the tailor Shoenfeld live here?" asked the secret agent.

"No."

"Who are you, then?"

"Shoenfeld."

"Why did you say that you didn't live here?"

"You call this living?"

* * *

Antonovich, the rich Russian landowner, summoned Bleustein, his business agent, and said to him, "Here are twenty-five rubles. I want you to buy me a dachshund."

"Your Excellency," answered Bleustein. "It's not possible to obtain a first-class dachshund for so small a sum. I will have to pay twice that amount. For fifty rubles I'll buy you a dachshund you can really be proud of."

"Here are twenty-five more rubles," agreed the nobleman. "But remember, it must be the best in all the land, as befits my station in life."

"Don't worry!" Bleustein turned to leave and then said, "Your Excellency, tell me, what is a daschund?"

* * *

At the market, Cohen, a Russian farmer, and his daughter sold all their produce for 500 rubles. As they headed back to the farm in their wagon a bandit stopped them. He searched the frightened couple then rode away taking the horse and wagon.

When the bandit had disappeared in the distance, Cohen began wailing, "Oh, Rebecca, I'm a ruined man!"

"Oh, no you ain't, Poppa," answered the girl.

"I lost my horse. I lost my wagon. I lost my 500 rubles, and now you tell me I ain't ruined!"

"Poppa, I saved the money!"

"You saved it? Where, Rebecca, where?"

"I put it in the cavity between my legs. Here it is."

"Wonderful!" cried Cohen counting the cash. "What a shame your mother wasn't here. We could've saved the horse and wagon."

* * *

Fogelman applied for a job as a lumberjack in the Canadian north. He had hoped to earn enough money to bring the rest of his family over from Austria.

"All right," said the foreman. "Here is an axe. An average lumberjack can cut down that 8-inch-diameter tree in six or seven minutes. Let's see what you can do."

In two minutes Fogelman chopped down the tree.

"I can't believe it," said the foreman. "The best lumberjack in Canada couldn't have done

* * *

that in less than four minutes, 18 seconds. Here's an 18-inch tree; no lumberjack alive can fell that tree in less than 18 minutes, 26 seconds."

Fogelman felled the tree in six minutes, 55 seconds.

"Your technique is unbelievable. Where'd you learn lumberjacking?"

"In the Sahara."

"In the Sahara? There ain't no trees in the Sahara!"

"Well, not anymore there ain't!"

* * *

Kovar, a Czechoslovakian secret policeman noticed Bloomberg hurrying through Prague with a suspicious-looking satchel under his arm.

"Hey, Jew!" he shouted. "What you got in the bag?"

Bloomberg opened the bag. It was full of banknotes.

"Where you get all that money?" asked Kovar.

"I'm a professional gambler. I won it on bets."

"I believe that if you prove you really gambler," said the secret policeman.

"All right, I'll bet you five hundred koruna that I can bite my eye."

Kovar accepted the wager. Bloomberg removed his glass eye and bit it.

"I still not satisfied," said the policeman. "You got give more proof."

* * *

"I'll bet you five hundred koruna that I can bite my other eye."

"Okay," said Kovar.

Bloomberg then removed his false teeth, bit his other eye and relieved the secret policeman of the money.

The communist cop was furious. "That be cheap trick," he shouted. "You still no prove that you professional gambler. I demand one more proof."

"I'll bet you five hundred koruna that I can piss in your boot and it will smell just like rosewater."

Kovar eagerly accepted. He took off his boot and Bloomberg urinated in it. The cop sniffed the boot. It smelt not of roses, but of urine.

"Aha!" said Kovar. "Now you pay me back five hundred koruna. You not so damned clever after all!"

Bloomberg paid back five hundred koruna and turned to go.

"Wait," said the secret policeman. "You must know you couldn't piss rosewater, why you make that bet?"

"Look at that crowd of people over there," said Bloomberg. "Each one of them bet a thousand koruna that I wouldn't dare piss in your boot."

* * *

In 1930 Ostrow decided to leave Germany and go to the Soviet Union, the working people's paradise. His friend Sulzberger had reservations about leaving.

"All right," said Ostrow. "I'll go first and write back and tell you what it's like. Then you can join me."

"Maybe they have censorship," said Sulzberger. "Look, if everything is all right, use regular ink. But if you want to convey to me that what you're writing is not true, then use green ink."

Ostrow went to Russia. Three months later Sulzberger got a letter from him.

"Everything is fine. There's plenty to eat and drink. I have a big apartment and two suits. Don't believe what you read about Russia—it's all lies. You can get everything you need here. The only thing you can't get is green ink. Sincerely, Ostrow."

* * *

A Jew was walking on a street in Berlin when he accidently brushed against a black-shirted storm trooper.

"Swine!" roared the Nazi.

"Plotnick," said the Jew bowing.

* * *

A working party returned to a concentration camp just after there had been an assassination attempt on Hitler.

"Heard any news?" said one prisoner.

"Yes, two things," replied his bunkm' "One good and one bad. Hitler's dead."

"What's the bad news?"

"It's not true."

* * *

Rick Friedberg, Hollywood's dynamite film director, delivered this delightful dandy:

The Nazis had taken over Denmark and the Danes went about their lives as best they could. One day a German staff car caught fire and a large crowd gathered to watch it burn.

Suddenly, Hirschberg appeared carrying a pail and a bicycle pump. He took the end of the hose, submerged it in the pail and then squirted it at the burning automobile. The flames continued to spread.

Once again, the Jew loaded the pump from the pail and sprayed it on the German vehicle to no avail. He did it once more but still the fire did not subside. A Dane tapped Hirschberg on the shoulder and said, "Do you think that does any good?"

"Oh, yes," said the Jew. "That's kerosene!"

* * *

Mueller and Heintz, two German judges were talking about their courts being empty.

"I haven't had a case in over a month," sighed Mueller. "I can't understand it."

"Well, I can," grumbled Heintz. "We haven't any work because a Jew will not sue another Jew, and he is afraid to sue an Aryan. An Aryan will certainly not sue a Jew because it would advertise the fact that he had business dealings with a Jew."

"That's true," acknowledged Mueller. "But still, one Aryan can sue another Aryan."

"No, they won't do that either," explained the other judge. "Where would they get Jewish lawyers to defend them?"

* * *

An American spaceship landed on Mars. An astronaut climbed down and was met by a friendly Martian. "Thank you for welcoming us," said the American. "Would you be kind enough to answer a few questions?"

"Of course," answered the Martian.

"Do all Martians have one red eye in the middle of the forehead?"

"Yes," answered the little man.

"Do all Martians have antennas growing out of your ears?"

"Yes!"

"Do all of you wear those funny, little green hats on your head?"

"Not the *goyim!*"

* * *

Malicious Mouthfuls

"A-ah, drop dead!" That remark in some segments of today's society is considered an acceptable invective. Of course, expressions of verbal abuse have long been part of the Jewish need to vent anger and frustration.

However, just a simple, "A-ah, drop dead!" falls short of the mark. It is not nearly clever, or creative or inventive enough. Here are some classic Yiddish curses from the old country you may recognize having been intoned by your grandparents:

You should become so poor that you have to go begging and you come to me for money and I hope I ain't got any to give you.

* * *

May you have to spend many hours in a soft chair—at your dentist.

* * *

May an oak grow in your left ear and the acorns burst your bellybutton.

* * *

May the lice in your shirt marry the bedbugs in your mattress and may their offspring set up residence in your underwear.

* * *

It should smell from your head like it smells from my feet.

* * *

May you jump up with joy—and right into an open manhole.

* * *

May you finally hear God's heavenly music and break your leg while dancing to it.

* * *

It should run from your nose like it leaks from my faucet.

* * *

May you turn into a centipede with ingrown toenails.

* * *

May you lose all your teeth except the one that aches.

* * *

May you have to spend your healthy days on your back and your sick days on your feet.

* * *

May your wife eat *matzohs* in bed and may you roll in the crumbs.

* * *

May your sex life be as good as your credit.

* * *

May your hat be the right size, but your head too small.

* * *

May you always bite worms while eating apples.

* * *

May the bird of paradise fly you to Hawaii
and drop you in a volcano.

* * *

May the day you were born be erased from the calendar.

* * *

May a rash cover your entire body as you leave your house today.

* * *

May all your relatives move in with you.

* * *

May you romp with joy and skid right into a sewer.

* * *

May the whole Atlantic become your enema.

* * *

May you become famous—in medical history.

* * *

May all your shoes be too long and your haircuts too short

* * *

May all your baths be too hot and your women too cold.

* * *

May your daughters be so famous every policeman knows them.

* * *

May your mouth never close and your *tuchis* never open.

* * *

May your wife be as much help to you as a lame horse.

* * *

May you bargain with God and lose.

* * *

May you break a leg and lose your crutch.

* * *

May your appetite enlarge and your digestion diminish.

* * *

May everything you cook stick to the bottom of the pan.

* * *

May you eat chopped liver with onion, pickled herring, chicken soup with *matzoh* balls, gefilte fish with horseradish, boiled beef with *tsimmes,* potato pancakes with applesauce, tea with lemon every day, and may you choke on every bite.

* * *

Teitelbaum, the hotel owner, was arguing with the egg farmer from down the road. "I ain't buying your lousy eggs," he shouted. "My hotel should burn down and I wouldn't buy them. My wife should die and I wouldn't buy them. My children should choke and I wouldn't buy them. My children shouldn't have children and I wouldn't buy them."

The farmer shouted, "You should go blind and buy a whole case."

"Listen," said Teitelbaum, "leave me out of it."

* * *

Jewish Polish Jokes

Humor historians disagree as to the origin of Polish jokes. Although using a specific minority as the butt of a gag is not new, poking fun at Poles seems to have stayed popular longer than any other type of put-down joke (except for two thousand years of anti-semitic humor).

There is a town in Poland, called Chelm. During the 19th century for some unaccountable reason, its mostly Jewish citizens symbolized innocent stupidity. Humorous stories about the fools and simpletons of Chelm began to surface, and soon these Polish Jews became famous wherever men gathered for drinks and joke telling.

Could this have been the origin of what we now call Polish jokes? You be the judge!

"Which is more important, the sun or the moon?" a citizen of Chelm asked the rabbi.

"What a question!" snapped the cleric. "The moon, of course! If it didn't shine at night it would be so dark we couldn't see a thing. On the other hand, the sun shines by day when it's already broad daylight!"

* * *

A fire broke out one night in Chelm and all the inhabitants rushed to the fiercely burning building to put out the blaze. When the conflagration had been extinguished, the rabbi addressed the citizens:

"My friends, this fire was a miracle sent from heaven above."

There were murmurs of surprise in the crowd.

"Look at it his way," he said. "If it were not for the bright flames, how would we have been able to see how to put the fire out on such a dark night?"

* * *

Lemburg the candlemaker was returning home one evening when a stranger rushed up and punched him in the face.

"Take that, Peretz!" yelled the attacker.

Lemburg picked himself up from the street and began laughing.

"Peretz, why are you laughing?" exclaimed the other. "I just knocked you down."

"The joke is on you," chortled Lemburg. "I'm not Peretz!"

* * *

Littner and Klamer, two Chelmites were taking a walk. Littner carried an umbrella with him. Suddenly it started to rain.

"Quick, open your umbrella!" said Klamer.

"It's no use," answered Littner. "My umbrella is full of holes."

"Then what the hell did you take it for in the first place?"

"I didn't think it would rain!"

* * *

A group of citizens were digging a foundation for the new synagogue.

"What are we going to do with all this earth we're digging up?" asked Horwich. "We can't leave it here where our Temple will be built."

"I got the solution," proclaimed Fischel. "We will make a deep pit, and into it we'll shovel all this earth we're digging up for the synagogue!"

"That won't work!" said Horwich. "What will we do with the earth from the pit?"

"Simple," said Fischel. "We dig another pit, and into that one we'll shovel all the earth we're digging now, and all the earth we take out of the first pit. The only thing we gotta do is be careful to make the second pit twice as large as the first one."

* * *

Itzik returned home from the County Fair and Vilnay, his neighbor, asked him if he had enjoyed the carnival.

"No," said Itzik. "The Fair should never have been permitted to come to Chelm. One of the guards spoke rudely to me and said they did not particularly welcome Jews."

"That's terrible!" agreed Vilnay. "What did you do?"

"I got my revenge," said Itzik. "I bought a ticket but I didn't go in!"

* * *

Howard Hinderstein, the humor-loving Hollywood theatrical rep hooks titters with this happy bit of hyperbole:

A thief broke into the Chelm synagogue and stole the poor box. The Board of Directors held a meeting and came to a unanimous decision. A new poor box would be installed, but hung close to the ceiling so that no thief would ever be able to reach it.

When the *shammes* heard about the decision he went before the board. "It is true that the box will be safe from thieves," he pointed out, but it will also be out of reach of the charitable."

The Directors held another hurried meeting, and once again, they reached a decision unanimously. It was decreed that a stairway be built to the poor box so that the charitable might easily reach it.

* * *

Hockman, the Hebrew teacher, and Luchinsky, the Rabbi of Chelm, were sipping tea and discussing the town's economy.

"There is great injustice heaped on the poor," sighed Hockman. "The rich, who have more money than they need, can buy on credit. But the poor, who haven't two coins to knock together, have to pay cash for everything. Is that fair?"

"Of course," answered Luchinsky.

"But, it should be the other way around," insisted Hockman. "The rich, who have money, should pay cash and the poor should be able to buy on credit."

"I admire your ideals," said the rabbi. "But a merchant who extends credit to the poor instead of the rich will soon become a poor man himself."

"So?" retorted the Hebrew teacher. "Then he'd be able to buy on credit, too!"

* * *

Motkele came home from the Chelm public baths without his shirt.

"Where is your shirt?" demanded his wife. "How many times must I tell you to watch your belongings?"

"Well," explained Motkele. "Someone else at the baths mistook my shirt for his so he took mine by mistake."

"*Nu,* then where is the other man's shirt?"

"He must have forgotten to leave his."

* * *

Gershon returned to Chelm after a two-day visit to the city where he bought goods for his little store.

"Hannah, it is good to be back among the poor people," he said to his wife. "When I travel among the rich I cannot help but notice that they are all selfish, greedy and dishonest, while the poor are very decent."

"I agree," said Hannah. "But, did something happen in the city to remind you?"

"Yes," answered Gershon. "After running all day long from one business house to another, I discovered that my walking stick was missing. I couldn't remember at which one of those rich places I left it. The next day I went to look for it. At the first place the millionaire owner denied ever seeing my stick. The second rich owner also said I didn't leave it there. The whole day I revisited all the rich places I had been and all the owners denied it. Finally, at night, I went to a poor little restaurant where I ate the evening before and without a word the owner handed me my stick.

"See, Hannah, that's the difference between the rich and the poor!"

* * *

A Chelmite was drowning and shouted, "Help! Help! I'm going under!"

A passerby on the shore heard the drowning man's pleas.

"Why are you making such a to-do?" he yelled back. "If you can't swim, why don't you at least get out and learn how?"

* * *

The synagogue's Board of Directors were faced with a dilemma. Suppose they caught a thief; what would they do with him? There was no jail in the town, and the crime of stealing was not serious enough to warrant exile from Chelm.

The seven Directors pondered the problem but made no progress until the rabbi came up with the solution: "Bore two holes in the bathhouse wall. Make the prisoner pass his hands through the holes and keep them there for as long as the judge decided was right and proper."

"No good," protested one Board member. "Suppose he should simply withdraw his hands and walk away before he had served his full sentence?"

"That's no problem," answered the rabbi. "Once his hands are passed through the holes he will be ordered to make a fist, so he can't withdraw his hands without unclenching them!"

* * *

Cazinsky, the young candlemaker of Chelm, married an eighteen-year-old girl and, three months later, she gave birth. He rushed to the rabbi for an explanation.

"Rabbi," he exclaimed, "my wife just had a baby, and we have only been married three months. My own mother told me it takes nine months to make a baby."

"We will solve this mystery with talmudic logic, son. You have been married for three months?"

"Yes, Rabbi."

"Your wife has lived with you for three months?"

* * *

"Yes."

"And you have lived with your wife for three months?"

"Yes."

"How much is three months plus three months plus three months?"

"Nine months."

"Correct," said the rabbi. "Now go home to your wife and nine-month baby."

* * *

The cantor of Chelm was about to marry off one of his daughters. He was a poor man so the Board of Directors advanced him two hundred zlotys to be deducted from his salary during the next five years. But the cantor was an honorable man and though he needed the money, he stood before the Directors of the synagogue.

"Gentlemen," he began, "please understand that I am accepting your kind help on the following two conditions: Should I live for five more years, that is your good fortune. However, should I die before the five years are up, that is my good luck!"

* * *

Tevya was milking his cows one morning when a disturbing thought crossed his mind. He immediately rushed to Chelm to ask the rabbi for an explanation.

"Rabbi," asked Tevya, "why are the summer days long, and the winter days short?"

"That's very easy to answer, my son," said the rabbi. "Summer is hot—therefore the days expand. Winter is cold, so the days get short!"

* * *

The first heavy snow fell one Friday afternoon and the Chelmites rejoiced to see the lovely white blanket covering their town.

But a sad not was struck by the rabbi. "The *shammes* will soon be passing through the town to call on the people to prepare for the *Shabbes*. He will leave ugly tracks in the beautiful snow when he walks on it."

The Directors of the synagogue were asked to solve the problem. They agreed, the snow must be kept trackless, no matter what. But how to prevent the *shammes* from tracking it up?

Suddenly the rabbi stood up. "I have it!" he cried. He explained his idea to the Board and they agreed to the plan.

When the *shammes* finally started on his rounds, he was made to stand on a table so that he might not make tracks in the pretty snow. And, in accordance with the rabbi's scheme, the table was carried through the town by the seven members of the Board!

* * *

Michelson, the winemaker murdered a fellow Chelmite. The Board of Directors convened and sentenced him to death.

A murmur of approval swept through the onlookers at the trial, but the *shammes* raised his hand to speak.

"I consider the sentence just," he began. "However, if you execute Michelson where will we get our wine? There is not another winemaker within forty miles of Chelm."

The patriarch of the Board nodded and then addressed the townsfolk.

"It is true Michelson, the winemaker is too valuable to our community to dispense with him. But justice must be done. Since we have two cabinet makers for Chelm and we need only one, it is decreed that one of them shall be executed instead."

* * *

Hayim and Yigal, two Chelmites, were in the coffee house sipping a glass of tea.

"It takes four hours to drive to the city with one horse, is that correct?" asked Hayim.

"Yes!" answered Yigal.

"So if I drove with two horses, doesn't it follow that I would cut the time in half—that it would only take two hours?"

"Absolutely logical."

"So, if it takes four hours with one horse and two hours with two horses, doesn't it stand to reason that with four horses I'd make the trip in no time at all?"

"Wait," said Yigal. "If it takes no time at all, why not just harness the horses and stay right here instead of making such a long trip?"

* * *

Mark Weissman, San Diego's super sports promoter, savors this satirical silly:

Herzl the cobbler went to the wisest member of the synagogue's Board.

"It is an established fact," began Herzi, "that whenever you drop a slice of bread it always falls butter-side down."

"That's true," agreed the Chelmic dignitary.

"Well, today I dropped my bread and it fell butter-side up!"

"The explanation is simple," said the wise man. "You should have buttered your bread on the other side!"

*   *   *

The wisest of the Chelm thinkers met every week for twenty years to ponder the philosphical question: From which end does a man grow? From his head up or from his feet down?

At one meeting, Teitel, the tailor announced, "I have solved the problem."

"When I was a boy my father bought me a pair of pants. I put them on and they dragged on the floor. But a few years later they were above my ankles. This led me to believe that a man grows from his feet down.

"That recollection provided me with an answer, but an incorrect one," continued Teitel. "But yesterday, the truth was revealed to me. A company of soldiers marched through Chelm yesterday morning. I noticed that their feet were all on a level, but some heads were higher than others, some lower. So we finally have our answer," he concluded, "a man grows from the head up and not from the feet down."

*   *   *

"Oh, learned one," ask Eckstein of the rabbi. "Why is the sea salty?"

"Because of the herring, my son!"

* * *

* * *

A traveler stopped at the Chelm tavern for dinner, and when he finished his meal he asked for the bill.

The owner, Mrs. Toretsky added up the costs: "The chopped egg, bread and soup comes to seven groszy," she said. "For the fish is another seven groszy. Altogether, eleven groszy."

"But Madam," corrected the honest stranger, "two times seven are fourteen!"

Mrs. Toretsky added up the sum again. "No," she repeated, "two times seven are eleven!"

"How did you arrive at that figure?"

"Like this: I was a widow with four children. I married a widower who also had four children. Then we had three children of our own. Now he has seven children and I have seven children, and altogether we have eleven. Two times seven are eleven!"

The stranger paid the bill and left Chelm shaking his head.

* * *

Paupers, Peddlers, and Pushcarts

During the early 1900's European Jews flocked to the shores of America fleeing from persecution and pogroms. In the new country they faced a different language, strange customs, and they were forced to fend with an unusual culture. The following stories reflect the humor of those early days in the United States:

Perlman, the peddler was sitting in his lawyer's office making out his will. "Put Elihu down for $20,000. Put Jerome down for $30,000. See that another $30,000 goes to Hymie. . . ."

"Just a moment, Mr. Perlman," said the attorney, "where is all this money to come from?"

"To hell with them," replied Perlman. "Let 'em work for it the way I had to!"

*   *   *

Slutsky owned a pushcart clothing business. One day he was hauled into police court and charged with obstructing the traffic.

Judge: What is your name?
Lou: Lou Slutsky.
Judge: Where do you live?
Lou: Mine residence iz in Hester Street.
Judge: What is your occupation?
Lou: De try coods peezeness; secondhand cloze.
Judge: What is your religion?
Lou: Don't say nothin', Chudge, I'm a Quaker.

* * *

Krebs, the *shnorrer* was a regular Sabbath dinner guest at the table of Brodsky, a rich and charitable merchant. One day, Krebs, the beggar showed up at the house accompanied by a young stranger and they both sat down to dinner.

"Who is that?" demanded the host.

"He became my son-in-law last week," replied the beggar, "and I agreed to furnish his board for the first year."

* * *

Seligman had recently arrived from the old country and was trying to sell some merchandise to an anti-semite. "I only buy from 100% Yankees," said the New Englander.

Seligman somehow convinced him that he was a 100% Yankee and sold him a large order. As Seligman was closing his sample case, he looked

* * *

up and saw on the wall pictures of George Washington and Abraham Lincoln.

"Fine-looking men," commented the refugee. *"Your partners?"*

* * *

Berger went to the "Big Man" on New York's Lower East Side. "Harvey, you're the big man here, I want you to do me a favor. I want to be an alderman!"

"You wanna be an alderman, all right, I'll talk to the committee."

Two weeks later, Berger was made an alderman.

In a year Berger came back and asked to be the mayor. They made him mayor. Two years passed, and he wanted to be Governor.

Harvey, the "big man" saw to it.

One day, Harvey went to the governor. "Listen, you wanted to be alderman, I made you an alderman. You wanted to be mayor, I made you mayor. You wanted to be governor, I made you governor. Now you gotta do *me* a favor. Make me a citizen."

* * *

A New York Immigration Officer discovered a form filled out like this:

Name: Gottleib, Hershel
Born: Yes.
Business: Lousy.

* * *

Steinberg sauntered into Gimbel's Department Store, took the elevator to the main office and met the owner. "I've been a peddler most of my life," said Steinberg, "and I made a few dollars and now I'm interested to buy your store. How much you asking?"

Gimbel decided to go along with the gag and said, "I'll consider 250 million."

"Could I use your phone?"

"Certainly."

Steinberg telephoned his wife. "Sweetheart, go down in the cellar behind the coal and take out the brown paper bag with the money it. Not the big one, the small one. Come right over to Gimbel's."

Mrs. Steinberg arrived with the bag and together they strolled about the store. Three hours later, Steinberg stood before Gimbel once more. "Well, I made up my mind," said the peddler.

"Yes?" smiled Gimbel.

"I ain't gonna buy."

"Why?"

"Because," said Steinberg, "there's no place to live in the back."

* * *

Katz and the missus received an invitation to a very high-class wedding and couldn't figure out the meaning of the initials R.S.V.P. "If only our son, the college grad, was here, he'd know," sighed Mrs. Katz.

Twenty minutes later Mrs. Katz shrieked, "Wait! I figured it out. R.S.V.P. means, *R*emember *S*end *V*edding *P*resent."

* * *

Rosenwald and his family were riding along the highway when he spotted a sign that said: "Be converted—Get $500." He stopped the car. Two hours later he came out of church with the money.

"I wanna new fur coat!" said his wife.

"I want a bicycle!" said his son.

"I want a doll!" said his daughter.

"You see," exclaimed Rosenwald, "as soon as we gentiles get a little money, right away, you Jews want to take it away."

* * *

Epstein met Madinsky on the street. "I haven't seen you lately," said Epstein. "Where do you live now?"

"I am living on One Hundred and Fifteenth Street now," replied Madinsky.

"What was the matter with that boarding-house on Fourteenth Street?"

"I couldn't stand the meals."

"Why?"

"Well, the foist week when I was there the cow died, and we had beef all week. The next week the pet calf died, and we had veal all week. The next week Mrs. Blum died, and I moved. I didn't want to take no chances."

* * *

Levi: Sara, before you take the boat for Europe, we will put your jewelry in the safe deposit vault.

Sara: But I want to wear my jewelry on the ship.

Levi: Don't be a dumbbell. Suppose you drown and your body is not recovered.

* * *

Marty Wogansky, the popular Atlantic City Hotel host, loves this whimsical whopper:

Hornstein went into an Automat and bought a herring to eat. He took the plate to his table and after looking at the herring's eyes, he didn't have the heart to eat the fish.

The next day, Hornstein went back to the Automat and bought a fish once again, but after looking at its eyes, he could not devour the herring.

The following afternoon he went to a Jewish restaurant on the Lower East Side and ordered a herring. The waiter brought him the order, and there was the same herring with the pitiful eyes.

The herring looked up at him and said, "What's the matter, you don't eat at the Automat anymore?"

* * *

While Finkel was waiting for his train at Grand Central Station, he noticed a scale which gave weight and fortune for a penny. He dropped a coin into the slot and a voice said, "You weigh 195 pounds. You are Jewish, and you're on your way to Chicago."

Finkel stood there dumbfounded.

Another man dropped a penny into the slot and the voice said, "You weigh 185 pounds, you're Irish and on your way to Denver."

Finkel tapped the man on the shoulder. "Are you Irish and you're going to Denver?"

"Yes," said the man. Finkel shook his head in amazement.

Just then a man got on the scale and the voice said, "You weigh 165 pounds, you're Italian and you're going to St. Louis."

Finkel said, "Mister, you Italian and on your way to St. Louis?"

"Yeah," said the man.

Finkel rushed into the men's room, changed his clothes, put on dark glasses, pulled his hat down, turned up his collar, sneaked up on the machine and dropped a penny in the slot. The voice said, "You weigh 195 pounds, you're Jewish, on your way to Chicago, and *shmuck!* You just missed your train!"

* * *

"Milton, come upstairs and practice on your beautiful new violin."

"In a minute, Ma."

Fifteen minutes passed.

"Milton, come upstairs and practice on your

148

beautiful new Stradivarius violin that cost fifteen hundred dollars!"

"In a minute, Ma!"

Another ten minutes went by. Then,

"Milton, come right upstairs and practice, or I'll come down and bust this lousy fiddle over your head!"

* * *

Wertheim went for his final citizen papers.

"Where do you live?" asked the judge.

"Who? Me?"

"Yes, you."

"On Avenue A."

"What do you do?"

"Who? Me?"

"Yes, you."

"I'm a tailor."

"How old are you?"

"Who? Me?"

"No, me!!"

"Well, Judge, I would say you were between fifty and fifty-five."

* * *

Back when Babe Ruth was the hero of every boy in America, little Sollie came running in to his grandfather and excitedly yelled, "*Zayde, Zayde,* Babe Ruth just hit his sixtieth home run."

His grandfather looked at him and said, "So, how's this gonna help the Jews?"

* * *

Sammy said to his father, "Papa, I want to go to Texas—I want to be a cowboy."

"Don't go," his father said, "they don't like Jews there."

But Sammy left on the train for the Lone Star state anyway. Three days later as he rode through Texas reading his Jewish newspaper, the train suddenly screeched to a halt. Three tall, husky men wielding six-shooters went through the train asking, "Is thar a Jew on this hyar train?"

Sammy yanked off his *yarmulkah,* threw his newspaper on the floor and slid down in his seat. The three Texans approached him and repeated, "Is thar a Jew on this hyar train?"

Sammy just tried to be inconspicuous. Finally the three men stopped in front of Sammy and one of them said to him, "Are you a Jew?"

Sammy, terrified, whispered, "Y-y-yes!"

"Come," said the Texan, "we need another man for a *minyan.*"

* * *

Jewish Engineering

Zimmerman took his son to the state fair. The youngster got on the parachute ride and was caught by the dangling ropes. When he was being pulled heavenward the crowd stood aghast as he hung head downward. Suddenly Zimmerman shouted, "Irving! Irving! Throw out some of our business cards!"

* * *

THE SMALLEST BOOK IN THE WORLD

The Complete Guide to Jewish Business Ethics.

* * *

A man went into Bronfman's Book Store and asked for a copy of *Who's Who and What's What* by Malcolm M. Malcolm.

"We haven't got that book," said Bronfman, "but we have *Who's He and What's He Got* by Dunn and Bradstreet."

* * *

Melnick, the biggest mortician in town, was complaining to a friend.

"Business sure is off."

"How bad can things be?" replied the friend. "All four of these caskets are occupied."

Just then two corpses sat up and Melnick's buddy turned ashen. "Don't get upset," explained Melnick, "they're just my partners trying to make the place look busy."

* * *

A guy who can sell American-made transistor radios in Japan.

* * *

Goldstein applied for a job selling sporting goods in Abercrombie & Fitch. The manager agreed to give him a chance. Two hours later the manager walked into the fishing-equipment section and observed Goldstein talking to a very distinguished gentleman.

"What good is one fish hook? They're only 50¢. Take 3 for a dollar—you'll always use them."

"All right," said the man.

"You're goin' on a fishin' trip, why should you use the old line? Take 50 feet of new line, you'll use it!"

"Okay," said the man.

"Look, you got new hooks, a new line, you're not gonna use the old pole. We got a special on a new type pole, only $86, you'll love it!"

The man nodded.

"Listen, you got a pole, line, hooks—how could you go fishing without a boat? We got a new boat, just big enough for one man and it's only $465! For that price how could you go wrong?"

"O.K., I'll take it!"

"Now you got the boat, how you gonna carry it to the lake? Ya' need a little carrier made special for the boat, it's only $850!"

"Yes, I need it."

"Now, for the best bargain in the store. You got hooks, line, a pole, the boat, the carrier—except you gotta have a car to pull it all. And we got a small car, made special for fishermen, to carry his equipment and it sells for only $8,500!"

"All right, I'll take it." He wrote out a check and left the store.

The manager had watched the entire transaction. "Goldstein," he said, "I've been in the sporting goods business for 35 years and I've never seen a greater piece of salesmanship. To think, a man walked in for a fish hook and you sell hiim over $10,000 worth of merchandise!"

"What are you talkin' a fish hook? He came in looking for a drug store. I said to him, 'Are you sick?' He said, 'No, my wife is having her period.' So I said, 'Your wife is sick for a few days, why don't you go on a fishing trip?' "

* * *

"Abe, I got a great business proposition for you. I could get you an elephant for $200."

"Are you nuts? What am I gonna do with an elephant?"

"Don't be a dummy. Where could you pick up an elephant for $200?"

"But I only got a two-room apartment. Where the hell am I gonna put an elephant?"

"Don't you recognize a bargain when you see one? Tell you what I'll do. I'll get you two elephants for $300."

"Ah, now you're talking!"

* * *

Sokolow went to see Rudnick, the realtor about renting a small store in a run-down neighborhood.

"I want $400 a month," said Rudnick.

This infuriated Sokolow but he thought he'd show Rudnick up for a cheapskate.

"I'll be more generous than you," he said. "I'll give you $425."

"I'm generous, too. You can have it for $375."

"No. I'll give $450."

"No. $350."

"No," shouted Solokow, "$475."

"No!" shrieked Rudnick. "We're old friends!" "I'll give it to you for nothing as long as I live."

"Make it as long as I live."

"Why? asked Rudnick.

"Because," said Sokolow, "I'm gonna take your proposition and when I do you're gonna drop dead."

* * *

SIGN IN CHICAGO CLOTHING STORE

These pants will look better on your legs than on our hands.

* * *

Customer: "How much are your twenty-dollar shoes?"

Gluckman: "Ten dollars a foot!"

* * *

What does a Jewish Santa Claus do?

He comes down the chimney, wakes up the children and says, "Well, children, do you want to buy some toys cheap?"

* * *

1st Partner: I don't like the new bookkeeper you hired. She limps and stutters.
2nd Partner: What of it?
1st Partner: Why did you hire her?
2nd Partner: So she'll be easy to identify if she steals.

* * *

Schneider applied to a finance agency for a job, but he had no experience. He was so intense the manager gave him a tough account with the promise that if he collected it, he would give him a job.

"This guy'll never collect it," he told his secretary. "It's that Temkin, the tiemaker who's owed us that money for three years."

Two hours later, Schneider came back with the entire sum. "Amazing!" said the manager. "How did you do it?"

"Easy," replied Schneider. "I told him if he didn't pay up, I'd tell all his other creditors he paid us."

* * *

Oh Dawn's Ron Rothstein, the toilet tissue titan, gets titters with this tidbit of tomfoolery:

The people of San Francisco were awaiting the ultimate catastrophe. Early in the day news flashed that at 4:00 P.M. an earthquake would rip open the heart of the city, churn the water of the bay into a seething maelstrom that would demolish every building and every living thing.

All were gathered on the heights for the appointed hour of death. Haggard faces anxiously scanned the west for the ravaging waters. Bloodshot eyes gazed piteously at the Coit Tower for signs of the first tremor that would destroy the beautiful city by the bay.

At 3:30 P.M. lovers stood clasped in each other's arms. Wives clung to white-faced husbands. Children clutched nervously at the hands of their parents. The multitude was tense with hopeless expectancy.

Suddenly through the crowd came Krastenfeld shouting, "Earthqveck in 30 minutes, folks! Get your opera glasses and Eskimo pies now!"

* * *

Slotkin was teaching his new son-in-law the jewelry business.

"Now this is my best money-maker," he said, pointing to a case of wristwatches. "They cost me sixty dollars and I sell them for sixty dollars."

"If they cost you sixty dollars and you sell them for sixty dollars, where does your profit come in?" asked the boy.

"That," said Slotkin, "comes from repairing them."

* * *

Herskovitz, a dress manufacturer from New York's garment district, had to make a business trip which took him through Jordan.

At the Jordanian customs check-in, an official frowned at the American. "Are you a Jew?" he asked.

"Of course not!" exclaimed the New Yorker.

"Well, what is your religion?"

"I'm a Seventh Avenue Adventist."

* * *

Briggins brought an old, cheap watch to the Josefthal Jewelry Store to be repaired.

"I sure made a mistake in dropping my watch," he said.

Josefthal looked at it and said, "No, you couldn't help dropping it, but you sure made a mistake picking it up."

* * *

Barry Kaye, America's Supreme Insurance Investment counselor, cracks up clients with this corker:

Two bank robbers hit a small bank in the Cleveland suburbs one afternoon and herded everyone into the vault at gunpoint. They gagged Goodman, the teller, bound him hand and foot and forced him to the floor of the cashier's cage.

Suddenly, Goodman began to gesture with his head that he wanted to say something. After stuffing the money into sacks, the robbers removed Goodman's gag.

"Gimme a break, fellas, will ya?" he begged. "Take the books along with you. I'm eighteen thousand dollars short."

* * *

AD IN HOLLYWOOD SHOW BIZ PAPER

Need Anything?
Renta Yenta

* * *

Blumenthal asked Schwartz, a clothing store proprietor, "How's business?"

"Not so good," said Schwartz. "It looks like a sure-fire proposition."

* * *

Smulowitz and Ornstein owned a little textile mill. The business was quite successful but they didn't keep up their taxes. IRS agents arrived at the office and found Smulowitz in.

"Mr. Smulowitz," said the first revenue man, "you people are doing business and failing to report to the government."

"What's to report?" he demanded.

"Well," replied the agent, "first we'd like to know about your dependencies, your family exemptions."

Smulowitz told them about Yetta, his wife, dependent number one, and all the trouble and aggravation she had been giving him lately. Then he got to his son, and described how Benny had got a girl in trouble and the problems it caused. Dependent number three, daughter Beatrice, a good girl, but no beauty, and how much she was costing him. Then there was the *shiksa* in the stockroom office who needed new clothes all the time, money to visit her sick mother . . . not famly, but still a drain on his finances.

The agent said, "Mr. Smulowitz, let's forget about all that for a moment and concentrate on the business itself."

"Like what, exactly?"

"Like, how much business you're doing, what the assets are worth, how much profit you made. . . ."

"Are you crazy?" screamed Smulowitz, "I don't even tell my partner that!"

* * *

Berkman and Cooper, two manufacturing moguls, were talking about a mutual acquaintance.

"I put him on his feet," boasted Berkman.

"You did?" exclaimed Cooper. "You got a reputation as the most hard-hearted man in town! Why would you put him on his feet?"

"Because he couldn't keep up with his payments. I repossessed his car!"

* * *

Rabinovich, Hirshkowitz and Bloom bought a vacant movie theatre and were anxious to turn it into a money-making proposition. The first order was to redecorate the shabby auditorium.

"Gentlemen," said Rabinovich, "I think we should re-cover these seats with a plastic material!"

"That's nice," said Hirshkowitz, "but why not go first class. I'd like to cover these seats with leather!"

"My dear partners," said Bloom, "what we need to cover these seats with is *tuchises!*"

* * *

Arthur Shenker, Jr., Vegas' dynamic Dunes Hotel exec., delivered this dash of drollery:

Jake and Sol were partners in ladies' ready-to-wear and business was not too good. In fact, it was so bad they decided one of them should kill himself so the company would get the insurance money. They drew straws and Jake won.

Sol jumped from the roof of their 37th Street office building. Down, down! Passing the 18th floor, he noticed what a competitor was doing and yelled up, "Jake! Cut velve-e-e-t . . . !"

* * *

The Weissberg-Steiner Brassiere Company partners were having a heated argument. "We just made the biggest mistake in our history," cried Weissberg.

"What happened so terrible?" asked Steiner.

"We just got back a hundred dozen black brassieres. They wanted size 34, we sent them size 38. What the hell we gonna do with a hundred dozen black 38's?"

"Whatta ya worried?" said Steiner. "We'll cut off the straps and sell them for *yarmulkahs!*"

* * *

Aronson and Doriff, two successful shopkeepers, were arguing over business ethics. "I'll tell you one thing," Aronson said, "there are lots of ways to make money, but there is only one honest way."

"What way is that?" asked Dorff.

"Just what I thought," snorted Aronson. "You don't know!"

* * *

CERTIFIED PUBLIC ACCOUNTANT

*A Jewish boy who stutters and can't stand
the sight of blood.*

* * *

At height of the recession Garfunkel, the
owner of a big shoe company, was summoned by
Wilson, the vice president of the local bank.
"About that loan of two hundred thousand," said
the banker.

"Mr. Wilson," interrupted Garfunkel, "what
do you know about the shoe business?"

"Frankly," said the bank executive, "nothing."

"Better learn it fast," said Garfunkel, "you're
in it."

* * *

Keen-witted CPA Ken Gerstenfeld tells about Greenblat calling all his creditors together to tell them he was going into bankruptcy.

"I'm into you guys for over five hundred thousand dollars," he told them. "Unfortunately, I can't pay a penny of what I owe anybody. If you want you could cut me up in little pieces and divide my body among you."

"I vote we do it," shouted one of the creditors. "I'd like to have his gall."

* * *

Did you hear about the traveling salesman who died and left an estate of five hundred hotel towels and two hundred hotel keys?

* * *

Customer: Look here; all the buttons came off this coat the first time I wore it!
Zoretsky: Of course. So many people admired that coat, that you swelled with pride and you busted the buttons off!

* * *

Pinter went into a bank one day and asked the cashier to discount his note. The teller said, "I can't discount that note unless you get someone you know, a responsible man, to endorse it."

"Well," said Pinter, "you know me, and you're responsible. You endorse it!"

* * *

The men were arguing as to who was the greatest inventor. One said Fulton, who invented the steamboat. Another declared it was Morse, inventor of the telegraph. Another contended for Edison. Still another voted for the Wright brothers.

Finally, one of them turned to Pincus, the pawnbroker. "Who do you think?"

"Well," said Pincus, "the man who invented 16% interest was no slouch."

* * *

Cooperman, the furrier was having a difficult time with a customer. Every time Cooperman thought he had the mink coat sold, the customer found one more reason to pass it up.

At last, the furrier thought he was about to close the deal.

"There's one more thing," said the customer. "What if I buy the coat and I'm caught in the rain? Won't it be ruined?"

"Look, lady," said the furrier, "did you ever see a mink carrying an umbrella?"

* * *

Al Meshekow, California's colossal fur coat creator, contributed this chuckler:

Berkman and Slutzky, two New York garment manufacturers, decided to try something different for their vacations: they joined an African safari. Somehow they became separated from their party and the two wandered in the thick jungle hunting for game. Suddenly, Berkman heard an animal behind him and yelled, "Slutzky, I'm afraid to turn around. What's behind me, a leopard or a tiger?"

"Whattya askin' me for?" shouted Slutzky, "I ain't a furrier."

* * *

Tannenbaum went to Rabbi Silvers with a distressing story of poverty and misery in the neighborhood.

"This poor widow," he said, "has four starving children to feed. She's sick in bed with no money for a doctor, and besides that she owes $700 rent for three months and is about to be evicted. I'm out trying to help raise the rent money. I wondered if you can help?"

"I certainly can," said the rabbi, "if you can give your time to this cause, so can I. By the way, who are you?"

"I'm the landlord," said Tannenbaum.

* * *

Robert Dachman, Chicago's Little City fund-raising wizard, amuses colleagues with this whimsical winner:

At Bonds for Israel money-raising dinner was held in the grand ballroom of the Waldorf Astoria. Over 2,000 people attended and near the end of the evening a man in the rear stood up and said, "My name is Isaac Lieberman. I am the President of The Lieberman Dress Company at 842 W. 35th St. We make dresses for $42.50 to retail at $80.00. I would like to donate $50,000 *anonymous!*"

* * *

Sidney got a job as a health-insurance sales-man. For his first prospect, he was given the name of a big corporation president. If the man bought a policy, Sidney was empowered to speed up proceedings by bringing back a urine sample for processing the same day.

When Sidney came back late that afternoon, he was carrying the signed policy and a large bucket.

"That's great," said the boss. "But what's in the bucket?"

"Are you kidding?" said Sidney. "I sold the company a group policy!"

* * *

Members of the Temple Men's Club were discussing what was the best business. Finally, Horowitz said, "Let's stop lying to each other. The whorehouse business is the best. They got it—they sell it—they still got it."

"What are you saying?" cried a horrified old man.

"What am I saying? I'm saying, no overhead, no upkeep, no inventory. Who can beat it?"

"Yeah, and it's all wholesale!" added an-other man.

* * *

Teitelman, a traveling salesman staying in a small-town hotel, called in the redheaded chambermaid, and without a word threw her on the bed and had intercourse with her.

Afterwards, the girl said, "How is it you Jewish salesmen never ask a girl, the way other fellows do? It's the same way with the last six Jewish salesmen. They just throw me on the bed. What's the big idea?"

Teitelman took her into the bathroom and opened the door of the medicine cabinet. Written in soap along the bottom of the mirror in Yiddish it said: *"Die royte shiksa trennt."* (The redheaded gentile screws.)

* * *

SIGN ON TAILOR SHOP

We'll clean for you. We'll press for you.
We'll even dye for you.

* * *

Milt Josefsberg, the talented TV producer writer, told this pearl at a party:

Sydenberg had been selling ribbons for over thirty years all over America. Everyone bought his line except Belson, the buyer of a large department store chain, who was a bitter anti-semite.

One day, Sydenberg approached Belson for an order. "Get out of here, you dirty Jew!" shouted the buyer.

"Listen," pleaded the ribbon salesman. "I'm retiring next month, you won't ever have to see me again. But I can't quit knowing there was only one man who didn't give me an order. Please, you gotta buy something from me."

"Okay," said the bigot, "I want some pink ribbon. But no longer than from the tip of your nose to the tip of your pecker."

Three days later Sydenberg showed up with eight truck loads of ribbon. The buyer was furious. "I told you all I wanted was ribbon from the tip of your nose to the tip of your prick!"

"That's right," agreed Sydenberg. "I forgot to tell you I was circumcised in Russia."

* * *

Glossary of Jewish Words

ALTER KOCKER—*old man*
BUBELEH—*dear child, darling, sweetheart*
DAVENING—*praying*
GAY AVEK—*go away*
GAY EN DRED—*go to hell!*
GOY—*non-Jew, gentile*
GOYIM—*several gentiles*
GOYISHE KUP—*gentile brains*
KADDISH—*a mourner's prayer*
KIBBITZ—*tease, gibe, wisecrack*
KLUTZ—*clod, bungler*
KUMPT ARYN—*come in*
KVETCH—*to complain*
MAZEL TOV—*congratulations, good luck*
MEIN KINDT—*my child*
MEZUZAH—*oblong container attached to front door-
jamb*
MINYAN—*quorum*
MIKVEH—*a community bath*
MOHEL—*a man who performs circumcisions*
PUTZ—*penis*
ROSH HASHANAH—*New Year*
SHABBES—*sabbath*
SHADCHEN—*a professional matchmaker*
SHAMMES—*a sexton of synagogue*
SHAYGETS—*a gentile boy*

SHMUCK—*penis; a jerk, a bumbling boob*
SHNORRER—*beggar*
SHISKA—*gentile girl*
SHOFAR—*ram's horn*
SHVARTZEH—*female black*
SHVARTZER—*male black*
SIDDUR—*prayer book*
TALLIS—*prayer shawl*
TISHA BOV—*holiday of fasting and mourning*
TSIMMES—*a side dish of sweetened fruits and vege-
tables*
TUCHIS—posterior, behind
TEFILLIN—*two long leather straps with tiny boxes
containing parchments of writings from bible; used
for morning prayers by orthodox men.*
YARLMULKAH—*skull cap*
YENTA—*busybody, gossip*
YESHIVA BUCHER—*literally: rabbinical student*
YOM KIPPUR—*Day of Atonement*
YONTIF—*holiday*
YORTZEIT—*anniversary of person's death*
ZAYDE—*grandfather.*

ABOUT THE AUTHOR

LARRY WILDE, the world's best known jokesmith, was born in Jersey City, spent two years in the U.S. Marine Corps and then graduated from the University of Miami, Florida, with a Bachelor of Arts degree. He started his career in show business as a stand-up comedian, playing the nation's nightclubs and theaters and appearing on television commercials and sitcoms. Mr. Wilde's 21 books (which include two comprehensive studies on the serious business of comedy, *The Great Comedians* and *How the Great Comedy Writers Create Laughter*) are now read in every English-speaking land as well as in six other foreign countries. With sales of over 4,500,000, his "Official" joke books have become the biggest selling humor series in the history of publishing. Larry Wilde, who has been making America laugh for more than 25 years, is married to a former Wyoming beauty queen. He and his wife reside in Los Angeles.

We Deliver!
And So Do These Bestsellers.

LARRY WILDE

Here's how to start your own Larry Wilde
humor library!!!